DevOps Adoption Strategies: Principles, Processes, Tools, and Trends

Embracing DevOps through effective culture, people, and processes

Martyn Coupland

BIRMINGHAM—MUMBAI

DevOps Adoption Strategies: Principles, Processes, Tools, and Trends

Copyright © 2021 Packt Publishing

Group Product Manager: Wilson D'souza
Publishing Product Manager: Rahul Nair
Senior Editor: Sangeeta Purkayastha
Content Development Editor: Nihar Kapadia
Technical Editor: Shruthi Shetty
Copy Editor: Safis Editing
Project Coordinator: Shagun Saini
Proofreader: Safis Editing
Indexer: Vinayak Purushotham
Production Designer: Nilesh Mohite

First published: July 2021
Production reference: 1100621

Published by Packt Publishing Ltd.
Livery Place
35 Livery Street
Birmingham
B3 2PB, UK.

ISBN 978-1-80107-632-6

www.packt.com

Contributors

About the author

Martyn Coupland is the head of DevOps at Transparity, a UK-managed service provider of Microsoft Azure and modern workplace services. He is responsible for the cloud management platform product and the development of DevOps within the organization. Martyn is a Microsoft MVP, a Microsoft Certified Trainer, and a DevOps Ambassador for the DevOps Institute.

About the reviewers

Deb Bhattacharya applies Agile and DevOps to make organizations more successful. Over 20 years, Deb has helped over 50 teams across 4 countries to be more Agile and to be more DevOps. Deb is passionate about that.

Deb's other passion is sports. When Deb was younger, he used to play professional Table Tennis. He won many tournaments, but most importantly, he coached tournament-winning table tennis teams. Deb still plays Table Tennis at club level.

Deb uses all his experience from his hands-on software development background and his sports background to transform teams to Agile and DevOps. The two passions nicely come together here.

> *I am thankful to Anand Athani, my delivery manager from some 20 years ago, when I was an engineering lead. I was writing the thesis for my master's and Anand suggested that I picked up Rational Unified Process (RUP). That was the beginning of my Agile journey. This learning and contribution is still going on.*

James Wasson is currently the platform services engineering lead at Enable Midstream Partners and is a certified DevOps leader. In addition, he serves as an Ambassador for the DevOps Institute. James has spent his career looking for ways to eliminate bottlenecks and increase flow using value stream mapping, automation platforms, and infrastructure as code. His background includes assisting and leading digital transformations at financial institutions, healthcare providers, education providers, and oil and gas providers.

Table of Contents

Preface

Section 1: Principles of DevOps and Agile

1

Introducing DevOps and Agile

Exploring the goals of DevOps	4	Continuous deployment	11
Deployment frequency	4	**How does Agile play a part in DevOps?**	**12**
Faster time to market	4	The Agile manifesto	13
Lower failure rates	5	Do Agile and DevOps work together?	15
Shorter lead times	5	Agile is more than Scrum	15
Improved recovery time	5	Dealing with unplanned work	15
Values associated with DevOps	**6**	What is Scrum?	16
Challenges solved by DevOps	**7**	Kanban	17
Addressing these challenges	8	Kanplan	17
		Mixing methodologies within organizations	18
Phases of DevOps maturity	**8**	Scaling Agile teams	18
Waterfall	9		
Continuous integration	10	**Summary**	**21**
Continuous delivery	11		

2

Business Benefits, Team Topologies, and Pitfalls of DevOps

Key business benefits of DevOps	24	Cost savings	25
CX	25	Boost in productivity	25
Business growth	25	Improved employee retention	26

Better-quality products   26
Higher customer satisfaction   26
Improved operational and process
efficiency   26

Transformation topologies   27

Development and operations
collaboration   28
Shared operations   29
DevOps as a service   30
DevOps advocacy   31
SRE   32
Container driven   33

Transformation anti-patterns   33

Development and operations silos   34
DevOps team silo   34
Development does not need operations   35

DevOps as a tooling team   36
Glorified SysAdmin   36
Operations embedded in development   38

Avoiding failed transformation projects   38

Rooting DevOps initiatives within
customer values   39
Management of organizational change   39
Failing to collaborate   39
Failing to adopt an iterative approach 40
Management of expectations in terms
of DevOps initiatives   40
Decoding failed DevOps transformation   41

Summary   43
Questions   43

3

Measuring the Success of DevOps

Common metrics used to measure success   45

Common velocity metrics   47
Common quality metrics   49
Common stability metrics   51

Designing metrics for your team   53

Scenario 1: Small organization with a
dedicated DevOps team   53
Scenario 2: Medium organization with
advocacy team   54
Scenario 3: Large organization with
numerous DevOps teams   55

Scenario 4: Small organization with
outsourced DevOps team   57

Creating rollups at an organizational level   58

Reporting when multiple teams work
on one product   58
Reporting when multiple teams work
on multiple products   59
Creating goals that are S.M.A.R.T   59

Summary   61

Section 2: Developing and Building a Successful DevOps Culture

4

Building a DevOps Culture and Breaking Down Silos

What is a DevOps culture?	66	Lack of buy-in	78
Roles and responsibilities workshop	66	**Breaking down silos in your organization**	79
Rules of engagement	68		
Retrospectives	68	Creating one vision for team collaboration	80
Why is culture important?	70	Working toward common goals with collaboration tools	80
Increasing transparency	71	Educating together, working together, and training together	80
Better communication	72		
Collaboration across teams	75	Communicating often	81
Maintaining a strong culture	76	Evaluating team compensation	81
Starters and leavers	76	**Summary**	81
Pushing too hard for success	77	Questions	82
Lack of innovation	78		
Cultural differences	78		

5

Avoiding Cultural Anti-Patterns in DevOps

Organizational alignment	84	Prioritizing culture	94
Resistance to change	85	Continuous feedback	94
		Automation	94
Understanding the roles of organizational change	85	**Excessively focusing on tooling**	94
Organizational change process steps	86	How much automation is too much?	95
Overcoming resistance	89	**Legacy infrastructure and systems**	98
Breakdown in communication	91		
Difficulty scaling up	92	Legacy modernization	98
Start with small teams	93	**Summary**	99
Encouraging skill development	93	Questions	99

Section 3: Driving Change and Maturing Your Processes

6

Driving Process Change with Value Stream Maps

Understanding value stream mapping 104
Going beyond DevOps for process improvement 105
Taking a look at value stream mapping diagrams 106

How does value stream mapping help? 110
Challenges of value stream mapping 110
Use cases of value stream mapping 111
Identifying and reducing waste 112

Analyzing differences between process maps and value stream maps 114
Which should I use? 116

Explaining an example value stream map 117
Creating a value stream map 117
Current state value stream map 120
Future state value stream map 121

Summary 122
Questions 122

7

Delivering Process Change in Your Organization

Eight steps for effective change 124
Identifying what will be improved 124
Presenting a business case to stakeholders 124
Planning for change 125
Identifying resources and data for evaluation 125
Communicating 125
Evaluating resistance, dependencies, and risk 126
Celebrating success 126
Continuously improving 126

Models for business change 126
Kotter's change management model 127

Rogers' technology adoption curve 128
The ADKAR model 129
The EASIER model 130

People effects of process change 131
Direct impact 131
Indirect impact 133

The common challenges of process change 134
Summary 136
Questions 137

8
Continuous Improvement of Processes

What is continuous improvement and feedback? 140

Building a continuous improvement culture 140
Understanding and implementing Kaizen principles 140
Building a continuous feedback culture 142

Techniques for continuous improvement and feedback 144

Continuous improvement processes 144
Additional continuous improvement techniques 146
The continuous feedback process 147

Additional continuous feedback techniques 148

Iterating changes to processes 149

Iterative design processes 149
Using iterative design 150
Benefits of iterative design 150

Keeping pace with change 151

Effective communication 151
Knowledge transfer 152
Access to subject matter experts 152

Summary 153
Questions 153

Section 4: Implementing and Deploying DevOps Tools

9
Understanding the Technical Stack for DevOps

What are the families of DevOps tools? 158

Collaborating 158
Building 159
Testing 160
Deploying 160
Running 161

How does tooling help the adoption of DevOps? 161

Choosing tools that facilitate collaboration 162

Using tools that enhance communication 163
Lean toward tools with APIs 164
Always encouraging learning 164
Avoiding environment-specific tools 165

Understanding the benefits of DevOps tooling 166

Increasing code and deployment velocity 166
Reduction of time to market for new products and features 167

Decrease in the failure rate of new
releases   167
Improving the mean time to resolution 167
Improvement in reliability metrics   168
Eliminating high levels of work in
progress and technical debt   169

**Understanding the obstacles of
DevOps tooling   170**

Lack of definition of DevOps outcomes 170
Inadequate knowledge of tooling   170
Evaluation of tools   171
The volume of tools available on the
market   171
Lack of tool integration   172

Summary   172
Questions   173

10

Developing a Strategy for Implementing Tooling

**Understanding architectural
and security requirements   176**
Why is enterprise architecture
important?   176
Why is information security important? 178
Understanding architectural
requirements   181

**Developing training plans to
help your team   183**
Why are training plans important?   183

How to develop training plans for
your teams   185

**Defining owners and processes
for tooling   187**
Identifying the owners of tools in your
organization   187
Mapping processes to tools   188
Making tooling part of process
improvement   188

Summary   188
Questions   189

11

Keeping Up with Key DevOps Trends

What is XOps?   192
Where did XOps begin?   192
Understanding the XOps landscape   193
Approach to XOps   195

**Understanding the DataOps
ecosystem   195**
Understanding processes involved in
DataOps   197

Understanding tools involved in
DataOps   198

**Understanding the DevSecOps
ecosystem   199**
Understanding processes involved in
DevSecOps   201
Understanding tools involved in
DevSecOps   203

Understanding the GitOps ecosystem 205

Understanding processes involved in GitOps 206

Understanding tools involved in GitOps 207

Summary 207

Questions 208

12
Implementing DevOps in a Real-World Organization

Understanding why organizations move to DevOps 210

Technical benefits 211

Cultural benefits 212

Balancing stability against new features 212

Increased effectiveness 213

Defining our fictional organization 213

Current operating model 213

Challenges that exist within the current model 214

Goals for the future 214

Walk-through of DevOps transformation 215

Having initial planning workshops 216

Establishing a DevOps Center of Excellence 217

Setting up governance of the transformation 219

Establishing an intake process 219

Identifying and initiating pilots 220

Assessment of current capabilities 220

Performing transformation exercises 224

Scaling out the DevOps transformation 232

Summary 233

Why subscribe? 235

Other Books You May Enjoy

Index

Preface

Every organization wants to adopt DevOps and as an IT professional, it is important to understand the fundamentals of DevOps and how it can contribute to the success of your organization. This book provides complete coverage of the steps needed to implement the culture, people, and process aspects of DevOps.

Who this book is for

This book is for IT professionals such as support engineers and systems engineers and developers who are looking to learn DevOps and for those who are going through DevOps transformation. General knowledge of IT and business processes will be helpful. If you are in a business or service role within IT, such as service delivery management, this book will also be useful for you.

What this book covers

Chapter 1, *Introducing DevOps and Agile*, introduces the concepts of DevOps and Agile, explaining what DevOps sets out to achieve and how Agile plays a part in DevOps.

Chapter 2, *Business Benefits, Team Topologies, and Pitfalls of DevOps*, demonstrates the benefits of DevOps and looks at the team topologies used for DevOps adoption.

Chapter 3, *Measuring the Success of DevOps*, shows how to use metrics to measure success in DevOps and use the correct metrics for the right scenario.

Chapter 4, *Building a DevOps Culture and Breaking Down Silos*, examines the culture of DevOps in more detail and looks at how to build a successful culture and break down organizational silos.

Chapter 5, *Avoiding Cultural Anti-Patterns in DevOps*, covers the challenges of building a DevOps culture.

Chapter 6, Driving Process Change with Value Stream Maps, goes into what value stream maps are and how to use them in your organization.

Chapter 7, Delivering Process Change in Your Organization, looks at how to manage and deliver process change in your organization in order to be successful.

Chapter 8, Continuous Improvement of Processes, introduces techniques for continuous feedback and how to iterate process changes.

Chapter 9, Understanding the Technical Stack for DevOps, looks at the pros and cons of the DevOps toolchain.

Chapter 10, Developing a Strategy for Implementing Tooling, shows how to develop an effective strategy for implementing tooling and addressing the training needs of your organization.

Chapter 11, Keeping Up with Key DevOps Trends, explores the latest XOps trends and their relationship to DevOps.

Chapter 12, Implementing DevOps in a Real-World Organization, puts together everything we have learned to look at the implementation of DevOps in the real world.

Download the color images

We also provide a PDF file that has color images of the screenshots/diagrams used in this book. You can download it here: `http://www.packtpub.com/sites/default/files/downloads/9781801076326_ColorImages.pdf`.

Conventions used

The following text convention is used throughout the book.

> **Tips or important notes**
> Appear like this.

Get in touch

Feedback from our readers is always welcome.

General feedback: If you have questions about any aspect of this book, mention the book title in the subject of your message and email us at customercare@packtpub.com.

Errata: Although we have taken every care to ensure the accuracy of our content, mistakes do happen. If you have found a mistake in this book, we would be grateful if you would report this to us. Please visit www.packtpub.com/support/errata, selecting your book, clicking on the Errata Submission Form link, and entering the details.

Piracy: If you come across any illegal copies of our works in any form on the Internet, we would be grateful if you would provide us with the location address or website name. Please contact us at copyright@packt.com with a link to the material.

If you are interested in becoming an author: If there is a topic that you have expertise in and you are interested in either writing or contributing to a book, please visit authors.packtpub.com.

Reviews

Please leave a review. Once you have read and used this book, why not leave a review on the site that you purchased it from? Potential readers can then see and use your unbiased opinion to make purchase decisions, we at Packt can understand what you think about our products, and our authors can see your feedback on their book. Thank you!

For more information about Packt, please visit packt.com.

Section 1: Principles of DevOps and Agile

In this section, you will gain a working understanding of the basics involved in DevOps, including the benefits, pitfalls, and tooling.

This part of the book comprises the following chapters:

- *Chapter 1, Introducing DevOps and Agile*
- *Chapter 2, Business Benefits, Team Topologies, and the Pitfalls of DevOps*
- *Chapter 3, Measuring the Success of DevOps*

1

Introducing DevOps and Agile

In this chapter, we'll introduce DevOps and Agile. We'll explore a few questions, including *What does DevOps set out to achieve?*, and *How does Agile play a part in DevOps?*. We'll also explore the values of a successful DevOps transformation and the challenges that DevOps solves for organizations. We will also learn how to build the four phases of DevOps maturity.

In this chapter, we're going to cover the following main topics:

- Exploring the goals of DevOps
- Values associated with DevOps
- Challenges solved by DevOps
- Phases of DevOps maturity
- How does Agile play a part in DevOps?

Exploring the goals of DevOps

The subject of DevOps is one that tends to prompt many different opinions on what it means and exactly how you do DevOps within your organization. The goals of DevOps and what it helps you achieve within your organization is also something that you will get different answers for from different people, depending on their experience, the industry they work in, and how successful those organizations have been at adopting DevOps.

For many organizations, you can define the following common goals of DevOps. These are goals that apply to most organizations:

- Deployment frequency
- Faster time to market
- Lower failure rates
- Shorter lead times
- Improved recovery time

Of course, your organization may be driven by different reasons and even for similar organizations, I would expect their goals to be slightly different. After all, while most organizations share the same challenges, how these challenges can be addresses and which of these challenges will result in the biggest gain in value will also differ, depending on the organization.

Deployment frequency

Improving the frequency at which you release or deploy software in your organization is often a key driver of the adoption of DevOps. We must start to change the way we collaborate and communicate within our organization to deliver value to our end users.

When developers and operations teams start focusing on the same shared goals, they start working together more effectively and deliver better value.

Faster time to market

Most organizations will compete with another for the services they provide. Having a faster time to market gives you a competitive edge over your competitors. With DevOps, you can work to increase value by reducing the amount of time it takes from idea inception to product release.

As a business, your value degrades the longer it takes you to release features to your product and the quicker your competition can get ahead of you. So, achieving a faster time to market is a key goal of not just DevOps but the business as well.

Lower failure rates

Every organization has failures, but with DevOps, you can, over time, expect to realize lower failure rates through teams collaborating with each other and communicating better with each other.

> **Tip**
> Cross-functional in DevOps denotes where people from different areas work together in one team.

DevOps gives teams the ability to work more closely and communicate more effectively. In mature organizations, it allows for cross-functional teams. The shared knowledge between these teams and the individuals within them and the greater understanding of each other's roles leads to lower failure rates.

Shorter lead times

Lead time is the amount of time between the initiation and completion of a specific task. In DevOps, this would be the amount of time between work starting on a user story and that story making it to release.

Tied hand in hand with faster time to market, shorter lead times is not just about your product but everything in the whole life cycle. This could be anything from planning where you capture requirements more effectively all the way to building infrastructure quicker than before.

Through slick processes, effective communication and collaboration, and high levels of automation, the lead times throughout your cycle will be quicker, leading to high performance within your team.

Improved recovery time

Of course, we all know that most organizations have **Service-Level Agreements (SLAs)** to measure the performance of key service-based metrics such as availability. However, how many organizations can tell you, on average, how long it takes to recover a service? Not many.

Having the level of collaboration that lets you discuss the reasons behind failures, understand them, and implement steps to prevent them from happening again is a sign of a mature organization. An organization that measures this metrics and takes steps to reduce them is an even more mature organization.

Downtime is lost revenue and reputational damage to your organization, so reducing that level of downtime is very important.

In this section, we have explored what the key goals of DevOps are and the business value behind the adoption of DevOps. Next, we'll take this further by looking at the values that make DevOps successful.

Values associated with DevOps

DevOps can be split into various pillars when it comes to transformation. That being said, if you wanted to take a high-level view of DevOps rather than one at a deeper level, you can talk about DevOps as four specific buckets.

These buckets are as follows:

- Culture
- People
- Process
- Technology

I firmly believe the order of these matters. While the ambition may be to work on tooling first, following the order set out here will ensure your organizations get much more value from their DevOps transformation.

> **Important note**
> Culture is one of the most important aspects of a successful DevOps transformation, even above the use of technology.

The importance of culture in DevOps cannot be overstated; getting the right culture in your organization enables you to drive in the right direction and get more value later in the transformation. You should also not underestimate the challenge of changing an organization's culture – it requires drive and executive-level support to be successful.

Next is people, the lifeblood of any business and any product. You must ensure that you have the right people to get the right culture to achieve the goals that have been set out by your organization, and those people must have the right skills to achieve this. As important as executive-level support is to DevOps, so is having the right people to execute it.

Now, we have process. The right-minded people will be the ones who can work with and drive your processes in the right direction, applying appropriate techniques to ensure your processes are fit for purpose in a DevOps world. To work together, you need to adopt some processes for continuous collaboration, such as plan, develop, release, and monitor. Finally, you need the ability to repeat those processes on demand to deliver maximum value.

Finally, technology. By this point, the work you have undertaken in your DevOps transformation should have gained incredible value for your organization, but by introducing technology, you can add yet more value. Through automation tools, your processes can now be run on demand, more frequently, and, importantly, with a level of idempotency. This means that results with the same input parameters should not change over time. This is the value automation brings over human execution.

In this section, we have looked at the values that make DevOps successful. Now that we understand what it means to implement DevOps, we will understand the challenges that DevOps will solve in our organization.

Challenges solved by DevOps

DevOps does solve many challenges in organizations. You need to be mindful that many of these challenges have existed for a significant amount of time, have become engrained in how people operate, and that it will take some time to unpick the different levels to achieve what you want to achieve.

Prior to the adoption of DevOps, organizations were ordered in functional teams and reported to line managers, siloed away from the wider business and often each other. If all the conditions were met for deployment, then code was moved through to the operations teams to deploy the application. All these teams, along with others, worked individually, in isolation, resulting in time-consuming activities that were repeated and results that were not satisfactory.

The challenges of DevOps can generally be explained by three statements, which are as follows:

- Developers are unaware of quality assurance and operations roadblocks.

- Quality assurance and operations teams are generally unaware of the business purpose and value of the product.

- As teams work individually, each team has their own set of goals, often in conflict with other teams' goals. This leads to inefficiencies.

The best example for the last point in the preceding list can be made using development and operations teams. The developer's priority is to release new features to the product quickly, while the operations team's priority is to keep the application available and performing highly. These two goals are conflicting, which leads to inefficiencies between those teams.

Addressing these challenges

These challenges are addressed in DevOps by making teams cross-functional, working in collaboration with each other and communicating about other's work and the end results. Overall, this approach increases the feedback's quality and resolves issues with existing automation.

In DevOps, most processes are continuous. With the help of feedback cycles to improve on what you already have, this gives you the ability to constantly mature and evolve your processes, thus learning from previous situations and becoming a more mature team.

> **Important ote**
>
> Addressing the challenges of DevOps is a time-consuming task; you should not expect instant results from a few days or weeks of effort. It will take many months to achieve the goals you have set out.

Now that we have understood the challenges associated with DevOps, it's time to look at the phases of maturity in DevOps and see how an organization will progress based on them.

Phases of DevOps maturity

Organizations should be looking to mature the more they process and adopt different DevOps best practices. This is known as maturity, and four phases are used to describe the phases of maturity in DevOps.

These phases are as follows:

- Waterfall
- Continuous integration
- Continuous delivery
- Continuous deployment

Throughout the cycle of DevOps transformation, organizations should move from waterfall toward continuous deployment, visiting each stage along the way. However, it is worth noting that waterfall is not always the starting point; some organizations start later in the phases.

During the transformation process, you will find that different teams gain maturity quicker than others. There are many factors for this, including the type of work that the team does, the processes they have to follow, and, to a degree, the level of automation and tooling they already have in place.

Waterfall

The term waterfall will be common to you if you have worked on projects in the past. Waterfall is a project delivery mechanism where tasks are completed in a sequential order to achieve a specific goal. It can also be used to explain a method of software development.

Where development teams write code over a long period of time, those teams then merge their code in order to release the latest version. In this case, so many changes have been made to the code base that integrating the new version could take months. This is because the code looks so different from the previous version.

Waterfall has been in the world of project management for a long time, and even with the adoption of Agile getting more and more popular, many projects are executed using the waterfall methodology successfully.

The advantages of using waterfall as a delivery method are as follows:

- Simple model to use and easy to understand.
- Rigidity makes it easy to manage; each phase has specific deliverables.
- In smaller projects, it works well as the requirements are well understood.
- Stages for delivery are clearly defined.
- Milestones are well understood.
- Arranging tasks with resources is simple.
- Processes and their results are well documented.

That being said, waterfall does have several disadvantages, as with all process models. Some of these disadvantages are as follows:

- No time for revision or reflection.
- High amounts of risks and uncertainty.

- Not a good model for projects that are complex and object-oriented.

- Poor model for long-term projects.

- No working software is produced until late in the project.

- Measuring success within stages is difficult.

- Integration is done at the end in a big bang, making identifying bottlenecks hard.

Agile addresses some of these challenges and together with DevOps, you can address a large number of the challenges described here.

Continuous integration

Continuous integration (CI) is the practice of quickly integrating newly developed code with the rest of the application code to be released. This saves time when the application is ready to be released. This process is usually automated and produces a build artifact at the end of the process.

The process of CI contains a number of steps, and these are critical to achieving CI, which is meaningful and efficient. Automated testing is the first step toward CI. Four main types of tests exist that can be automated as part of CI. These tests are as follows:

- **Unit tests**: Tests that are narrow in their scope. They usually focus on a specific part of code, such as the method of a function, and is used to test the behavior of a given set of parameters.

- **Integration tests**: Ensures that different components work together. This can involve several parts of your application, as well as other services.

- **Acceptance tests**: In many ways, this is similar to integration tests. The big difference is that acceptance tests focus on the business case.

- **User interface tests**: Tests that focus on how the application performs from a user's perspective.

> **Important note**
> One vitally important element of CI is that you integrate early and integrate often.

When you integrate early and often, you reduce the scope of changes, which, in turn, makes it easier to identify and understand conflicts when they occur. Another big advantage of this approach is that sharing knowledge is easier as the changes are more digestible than big bang sets of code changes.

Another note is that if the main branch becomes broken by a commit in code, then the number one priority is fixing it. The more changes that are made to the build while it's broken, the harder it will become to understand what has broken it.

Every new piece of work that you implement should have its own set of tests. It's important to get into this habit of writing granular tests and aiming for a level of code coverage, as this gives you a comfortable level of knowledge that you are testing the functionality of your application sufficiently.

The value of CI is realized when the team makes changes on a frequent basis. It's important to make sure that your team integrate these changes daily. Integrating often, as you may recall, is key to making sure we can easily identify what is broken.

Continuous delivery

Continuous delivery (**CD**) is an approach where teams release products frequently and with high quality, and with a level of predictability from source code repositories through to a production environment using automation. It builds on the work that's done in CI to take the build artifact and then deliver that build to a production environment.

CD is, in fact, a collection of best practices associated with Agile. It focuses your organizations on developing a highly streamlined and automated software release process. At the core of the process is an interactive feedback loop.

This feedback loop, sometimes referred to as continuous feedback, centers around delivering software to the end users as quickly as possible, learning from experience, and then taking that feedback and incorporating it into the next release.

CD is a separate process to CI, but they chain off each other and in mature organizations, they are used together. This means that on top of the work you have done in CI to attain levels of automated testing, you can now automatically deploy all those changes after the build stage.

With CD, you can decide on a schedule that best suits your organization, whether that's daily, weekly, or monthly – whatever your requirements may be. If you want to get the true benefits of CD, then deploy to production as soon as possible to make sure that you release small batches that are easy to solve in case of problems that may arise.

Continuous deployment

Continuous deployment is one step beyond continuous delivery. Every change that passes through all the stages of your production pipeline is released to your customers. There is no human intervention – a failed test, at this stage, will prevent new releases to production.

Continuous deployment is a great way to speed up the feedback loop and take the pressure off as there is no release day. Developers are then able to focus on building high quality software while seeing their work go live minutes after they've finished working on it. Continuous integration is part of both continuous delivery and continuous deployment. Continuous deployment is very similar to continuous delivery; the difference is that releases take place automatically:

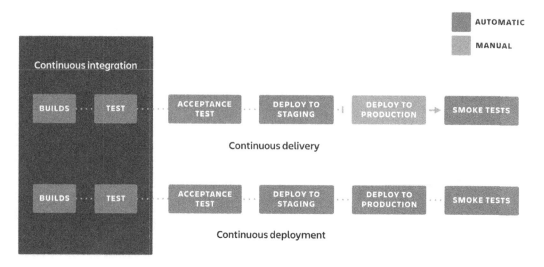

Figure 1.1 – Showing the differences between continuous integration, delivery, and deployment

In this section, we have looked at the major phases of maturity in DevOps. Armed with this information, we can now look at how Agile plays a role in DevOps.

How does Agile play a part in DevOps?

It is common to confuse the terms Agile and DevOps. Both are used together frequently and can be used interchangeably, but they are mutually exclusive terms. Where DevOps is the practice of bringing together development and operations teams, Agile is an iterative approach that focuses on collaboration, feedback, and small rapid releases.

While both are exclusive, you will find that, by the short comparison provided previously, the goals and values of DevOps are those of Agile as well. Agile is a key part of DevOps. While Agile focuses on constant changes and making developers and development cycles more efficient, DevOps brings in the operations teams to enable continuous integration and continuous delivery.

As a project delivery framework, Agile helps address some of the disadvantages of waterfall. It would be very difficult, if not impossible, to implement DevOps using waterfall practices due to the practices of continuous integration, continuous deployment, and continuous delivery. This is one major reason why, in organizations that practice DevOps well, teams use Agile as a delivery method.

The Agile manifesto

In 2001, 17 people met in the Wasatch Mountains in Snowbird, Utah. Their aim was to discuss the future of software development. What followed was an agreement on the frustration of the current situation of software development, even if the group could not agree on how to resolve the situation.

The group agreed that organizations were too focused on planning and documenting their software development cycles, which meant organizations lost focus and sight of what was important: customer satisfaction.

Most organizations discuss corporate values such as excellence and integrity, but these values have done nothing to foster people toward a better way of working, especially software developers. This was something that needed to change. Several members of the Snowbird 17, as they came to be known, already had ideas about how to revolutionize software development and start a new era. This trip to the mountains was the group's chance to define this new era.

What came out of this trip was the Agile manifesto. At just 68 words, this short and sweet document changed software development forever. The publication of the 12 principles defined in the manifesto has arguably led to the biggest change in software development. In the two decades that have followed, these 12 principles have been embraced by individuals, teams, and organizations around the world.

Defining culture

The Agile landscape is cluttered with ideas that seem to take Agile and transform them into real-world scenarios. This isn't anything new, though; in fact, the manifesto was born out of the need to find some common ground between Scrum, Crystal Clear, Extreme Programming, and other frameworks.

One of the biggest goals of the Snowbird 17 was to see if the representatives of these frameworks could agree – they did. The agreement ended up as a set of values that define a culture.

The Agile manifesto defines the following set of values:

- Individuals and interactions over processes and tools
- Working software over comprehensive software
- Customer collaboration over contract negotiation
- Responding to change over following a plan

You can look at the full manifesto that came out of the meeting in the mountains on the Agile Manifesto website at `http://Agilemanifesto.org/`.

Another product of the summit was the 12 principles (`https://agilemanifesto.org/principles.html`), which adhere to these values. They expand on the preceding four sentences that make up the values.

These 12 principles are as follows:

- Our highest priority is to satisfy the customer through early and continuous delivery of valuable software.
- Welcome changing requirements, even late in development. Agile processes harness change for the customer's competitive advantage.
- Deliver working software frequently, from a couple of weeks to a couple of months, with a preference for a shorter timescale.
- Businesspeople and developers must work together daily, throughout the project.
- Build the project around motivated individuals. Give them the environment and support they need and trust them to get the job done.
- The most efficient and effective method of conveying information to and within a development team is face-to-face conversation.
- Working software is the primary measure of progress.
- Agile processes promote sustainable development. The sponsors, developers, and users should be able to maintain a constant pace indefinitely.
- Continuous attention to technical excellence and good design enhances agility.
- Simplicity – the art of maximizing the amount of work not done is essential.
- The best architectures, requirements, and designs emerge from self-organizing teams.
- At regular intervals, the team reflects on how to become more effective, then tune and adjust their behavior accordingly.

Even if you had very little exposure to Agile and DevOps before reading this book, in those 12 principles, I hope you can see the connection between what we have explored so far and the principles of the Agile manifesto.

Do Agile and DevOps work together?

Agile and DevOps can sound like very different concepts. In fact, most people I speak to in the early stages of transformation are very confused by the idea of both. This confusion is also compounded as both have their own jargon and slogans. It is common for people to become frustrated with the plethora of definitions for DevOps.

Most people think that when you say Agile, you mean Scrum, and that when you say DevOps, you really mean continuous delivery. This simplification then creates tension between Agile and DevOps, to the degree that you would be forgiven for not realizing that Agile and DevOps are friends.

It was back in 2008, at the Agile Conference, that a session about Agile Infrastructure by Patrick Debois and Andrew Clay Schafer was undertaken, and the connection to DevOps was born. Patrick later coined the term DevOps, and the Agile Conference continues with a DevOps track to this day.

There is more to this than history, though. Now, let's look at the practical connections between Agile and DevOps by looking deeper than Scrum and continuous delivery.

Agile is more than Scrum

At the point when the limitations of the business or the work itself request something else, a deft group will use the basic standards of Scrum, review their practices, and adjust them to turn out to be more viable. This is especially significant when Scrum is applied external to the setting of programming advancement.

Dealing with unplanned work

In the DevOps people group, those with Agile experience recognize that Scrum is helpful for following arranged work. Some work in activities can be arranged: delivering a major framework change, moving between server farms, or performing framework overhauls. In any case, a large part of crafting tasks is spontaneous: execution spikes, framework blackouts, and traded off security. These occasions request quick reaction. There's no longer an ideal opportunity to trust that the things will be organized in excess or for the following run arranging meeting. Consequently, numerous groups that have come to grasp DevOps thinking look past Scrum to Kanban. This encourages them track the two sorts of work and causes them to comprehend the interaction between them. Then again, they embrace a cross-breed approach, frequently called Scrumban or Kanplan (Kanban with an accumulation).

From various perspectives, the way into Scrum's wide appropriation might be that it endorses no specialized practices. Scrum's lightweight administration rehearses frequently have a major effect on a group. Where there was once contending needs from different experts, there is currently a solitary arrangement of needs in the overabundance. What's more, where there was once an excessive amount of work in advancement, there is currently an arrangement that's obliged by what time has demonstrated is truly conceivable. In the mix, these can take a group higher than ever in terms of efficiency. Be that as it may, the group may wind up obliged due to the absence of specialized practices, such as coding audits, computerized acknowledgment tests, and persistent joining.

Other Agile cycles such as Extreme Programming have solid feelings about how specialized practices uphold the group's capacity to keep an economical movement and give straightforwardness and perceivability to executives and partners. Some Scrum groups resort to placing specialized undertakings in this overabundance. While that fits well for the direction of Scrum, it rapidly hits the handy issue of Product Owner inclination toward highlights. Unless the Product Owner is very specialized, she or he might not have the right stuff to assess the cost/advantage of specialized practices. That gets much harder for a Product Owner as the specialized assignments stretch into tasks to help unwavering quality, execution, and security.

What is Scrum?

Scrum is a system that assists groups with cooperating. Scrum urges groups to learn through encounters, self-coordinate while dealing with an issue, and consider their successes and misfortunes to constantly improve.

While the Scrum I'm discussing is most often utilized by programming improvement groups, its standards and exercises can be applied to a wide range of cooperation. This is one reason Scrum is so well-known. Regularly considered as a coordinated venture of the board system, Scrum depicts a bunch of gatherings, apparatuses, and jobs that work together to help groups structure and deal with their work.

Applying Scrum within your organization is no easy task and you will come up against a whole new set of terminology. Here is a short list, which is by no means exhaustive:

- Sprints
- Sprint planning
- Ceremonies
- Backlog

- Retrospective
- Standups

While Scrum is probably one of the most common frameworks in Agile, many others do exist. Kanban and Kanplan, for example, as we will discuss next, are useful for organizations that are new to Agile.

Kanban

Kanban is a well-known structure that's used to execute Agile and DevOps programming advancement. It requires continuous communication of work limits and provides a clear view of work which is planned, in progress, and completed.

Kanban works by placing work on a physical or digital board. This visualization enables you limit work in progress and maximize your efficiency, sometimes referred to as the flow of your teams.

Many people use a form of Kanban board for their everyday work. In fact, I know plenty of people who use one for everyday common tasks around the home. The board is split into various columns, and these columns define the different statuses of tasks.

Your Kanban board will also define limits around work in progress items, delivery points, and commitment points.

Kanplan

You may not have heard of the term Kanplan before. It is a mixture of methodologies, but something that may be right for your team.

> **Important note**
>
> When it comes to picking an Agile framework for your team, there is no silver bullet. Different methodologies in the framework have pros and cons based on many different parameters. Every team will need to determine which framework will work best for them when it comes to planning, tracking, and releasing software.

Kanplan combines features from both Scrum and Kanban. It is ideal for teams who want the ability to groom their backlog, but do not have the ability to work in sprints. It provides a great mix because teams cannot always apply the whole of Scrum, including sprints, but can quite easily work with Kanplan to start getting a better handle on their work, work in progress, their backlog, and the priority of the work in that backlog.

Mixing methodologies within organizations

There is nothing wrong at all with different teams adopting different methodologies of the Agile framework, mixing them together, and making it work for them. I've not worked with any organization who can simply lift something out of an Agile textbook and implement it in their organization.

Think of operational teams who cannot work with traditional Scrum, mostly because their work contains elements of unplanned work such as incidents. For them, Kanban works well as it puts no emphasis on planning. Think of a full DevOps teams working on a product within your organization. Here, the normal approach of Scrum would work for them as everything is within their control and they have no reliance on external teams.

Finally, think of engineering teams who want to be more Agile, but work with other teams who do not practice any level of Agile. This is a tricky situation as there is a need to be more Agile to deliver better quality but no appetite in the rest of the organization to adopt Agile methodologies. In this example, Kanplan would work well for them, giving them the ability to groom a backlog of work based on priority, then work in a Kanban-style board, which enables them to visually see work, work in progress limits, and work done.

This approach is a great starting point for teams who fit this description, and it will enable them to work toward a higher quality of work, integrating some of the technical methods of DevOps without needing the rest of the organization to follow suit.

Scaling Agile teams

Through what we've learned so far, we can see how implementing Agile in our organization can provide several benefits. However, organizations are bigger than individual teams, and you may have several teams working on one product. It is at this point that we need to understand how Agile can be scaled up to many teams within one organization. As opposed to implementing Agile at an individual team level, which is relatively easy, implementing across the organization is a real challenge.

Scaling Agile at an enterprise level requires that we adopt Agile concepts, as well as Lean-Agile at a functional level. This includes finance, procurement, HR, and sales, for example. At the enterprise level, Agile is practices being implemented across many teams and lots of engineers working in a portfolio manner.

> **Important note**
> Scaling Agile in the enterprise requires you to think functionally. So far, what we have explored is at a team level. To scale Agile, you must think of it as an organization-wide effort.

Netflix coined the phrase *highly aligned, loosely coupled*, and you can still see this phrase on their main jobs page. It describes a highly mature organization that uses Agile development across the whole enterprise.

Two models that are highly popular when it comes to scaling Agile at the enterprise level are the **Scaled Agile Framework** (**SAFe**) (`https://www.scaledagile.com/enterprise-solutions/what-is-safe/`) and the Spotify model for scaling Agile in the enterprise (`https://www.atlassian.com/agile/agile-at-scale/spotify`). Both are very popular, so let's look at them both in more detail.

Scaled Agile Framework

Taken directly from the SAFe website, this is the definition of SAFe:

> *"Scaled Agile Framework (SAFe) empowers complex organizations to achieve the benefits of Lean-Agile software and systems development at scale."*

The framework defines four core values:

- Alignment
- Built-in quality
- Transparency
- Program execution

SAFe is actually pretty broad and covers four primary areas: Agile development, lean product development, systems thinking, and DevOps. However, its core places more value on the four values described in the preceding list.

Alignment is needed to ensure you keep pace with changes that are happening fast, disruptive competitive forces, and geographically dispersed teams. Alignment is key in these scenarios since Agile teams are great, but strategy and alignment does not and cannot rest with opinions from all the Agile teams. Alignment comes from enterprise-level business objectives.

The larger the system, the higher the quality. There can be no argument as to the importance of quality, especially in large systems. Built-in quality ensures that every element in the overall solution reflects the quality that's required over the entire life cycle of development. You can think of this with Agile testing, **behavior-driven development** (**BDD**), and **test-driven development** (**TDD**).

Transparency stems from the fact that it is difficult to develop solutions. As things go wrong or do not go as planned, without a high level of transparency, the facts become obscure, and any decision-making process will not be based on actual data where the best decisions are taken. Building trust takes time, however, and transparency is a source of trust, which is provided at several levels through SAFe. Above all, none of this matters if the teams are unable to perform or deliver value on an ongoing basis. SAFe places a strong focus on working systems and the business outcomes. We know that while many organizations begin transforming with individual teams, they become frustrated as these teams then struggle to deliver more value reliably and efficiently.

Spotify model for scaling Agile

With a large number of globally distributed engineers, a key part of the success of Spotify is the company's approach to ensuring work is organized in a way that enhances agility. Throughout the journey that engineering teams at Spotify have gone through, this has been documented and shared with the rest of the world.

This model, now known as the Spotify model, is a people focused approach that focuses on autonomy for scaling Agile, with a strong focus on network and culture. Over the years, this has helped Spotify and many other organizations increase their levels of innovation and productivity by focusing on autonomy, communication, collaboration, accountability, and quality, but overall, delivery.

> **Important note**
>
> While commonly known as the Spotify model, it's not a framework. This is simply Spotify's view of how to scale Agile from both a cultural and technical perspective. It is one example of how to organize multiple teams in a product environment.

First introduced in 2012 (`https://blog.crisp.se/wp-content/uploads/2012/11/SpotifyScaling.pdf`), the model has been subject to much scrutiny from experts in the field. Upon inspection, it shows the radically simple way that Spotify has approached levels of agility. Since then, it's generated a large amount of buzz and became popular.

The overarching theme is the championing of team autonomy, and it has several ways of describing the structure of your organization. It does so by using the following terms:

- Squads
- Tribes
- Chapters
- Guilds

Squads are teams that are organized into Tribes, Chapters help subject matter experts keep in touch with each other, and Guilds are there to help people keep aligned across the whole organization, where Chapters enable you to keep together within a single Tribe.

> **Important note**
> Like any other Agile model, it's important to make sure that if you implement it within your organization, you have the feedback and transparency in place to generate and sustain a culture of trust and autonomy.

Now that we understand what role Agile has to play in DevOps, we know it's central to DevOps in so many ways and that it is vitally important if we want to succeed.

Summary

That concludes this first chapter. So far, we have introduced some terminology we will be using throughout the rest of this book and ensured you have a good foundational understanding of the main concepts of DevOps, the values it brings to your organization, the challenges it can help you solve, and looked at how Agile plays a part in DevOps.

In the next chapter, we will be taking a look at how the business benefits from DevOps, as well as looking at various team topologies you can use, depending on your structure, to achieve great things, as well as highlight some of the pitfalls of DevOps and how to avoid them.

2
Business Benefits, Team Topologies, and Pitfalls of DevOps

The ability to demonstrate how DevOps can benefit your business is important when it comes to driving the changes required to succeed. This chapter looks at the business benefits of DevOps transformation, as well as the team topologies that can be used during DevOps transformation. Finally, this chapter looks at pitfalls and mistakes that can lead to the failure of DevOps transformation projects.

In this chapter, we're going to cover the following main topics:

- Key business benefits of DevOps
- Transformation topologies
- Transformation anti-patterns
- Avoiding failed transformation projects

Key business benefits of DevOps

When it comes to DevOps transformation, buy-in from your executive leaders and senior management within your organization is fundamental. You will come up against serious challenges in your transformation without this support, and may even fail before you've really got started.

One way to ensure you have the required buy-in is by making sure that executive leaders and senior management understand what the business benefits of DevOps are. You cannot simply explain the technical or local benefits to individual teams or leaders. They will want to know why this is worth the money they will spend on implementing this new way of working and how it will help the business move faster.

In short, how can you ensure that DevOps addresses the **key performance indicators (KPIs)** and business goals of your organization?

> **Important note**
>
> When starting out with DevOps transformation, look to gain executive support early in the process; that way, you can change your approach if needed, based on your discussions with executives and senior leaders.

In order to best prepare for your meetings with senior leaders to discuss DevOps transformation with them, you first need to understand what the business goals are. This isn't at a high level; this is at a performance measurement level—what things are the business specifically looking for to turn the dial on their performance dashboards? These are areas you can look at in terms of how DevOps can help drive those KPIs within the business, such as the following:

- **Customer experience (CX)**
- Business growth
- Cost savings
- Boost in productivity
- Improved employee retention
- Better-quality products
- Higher customer satisfaction
- Improved operational and process efficiency

Let's now look at these elements in more detail to understand them better.

CX

In any business, customers drive success, and a better CX ultimately drives renewals of products and drives growth in the business. CX is vitally important to the success of any business. Improving the overall CX can boost things such as customer loyalty, retention, and profits, and can shorten sales cycles.

In DevOps, improved production support is key and is one of the foundational pillars of why DevOps exists. This better collaboration between development teams and operations teams often ends up in a boost in the quality of the product. It is these elements that have a direct impact on CX.

This alone ends up providing a huge boost in CX as the business and technical teams are focused on optimal output or—rather—the same goal.

Business growth

As sales and customer service grow, so do the prospects. In particular, there is a lot more capital to work for a company with improved growth. This money can be rolled back into the business in order to further develop processes and systems. In addition, increased productivity and performance ensures that workers have more time and can be freed to work on more efficient, revenue-generating projects.

Cost savings

It should be noted that all of the changes and enhancements listed here help to reduce overall costs. Improved production and performance result in higher sales, lower operating costs, and higher customer satisfaction ratings, which in themselves further improve revenue. DevOps explicitly encourages a continuous cycle of change and development.

Boost in productivity

More engaged and loyal workers means higher productivity rates, particularly if they believe in what they do. But it's more than just that factor that leads to improved productivity.

In **Information Technology (IT)**, teams are usually asked to do more with less money, which is where automation tools come into play. They can automate and refine internal processes that are repetitive and frequently rotate. DevOps honors this approach, even though it is extended to other areas of the market. Automating typical tasks frees up time for the workers, allowing them to concentrate on more meaningful tasks and spend more time on what they do.

Improved employee retention

Hands down, employee engagement is one of the most critical contributors to the success of an organization. If your workers are not satisfied, efficient, and compliant in their jobs, both performance and overall outcomes will suffer.

High-performance and functional DevOps work environments are proven to greatly enhance employee experience. The trend encourages higher employee engagement and productivity, but also increases brand loyalty. And when your current workers are satisfied, this bodes well for retention rates and invites new talent to come your way.

While a little obsolete now, Puppet's 2016 *State of DevOps Report* (`https://puppet.com/resources/whitepaper/2016-state-of-devops-report`) showed that promoters operating in DevOps-based organizations were 2.2 times more likely to recommend their business to a friend than those of low-performing DevOps firms.

Better-quality products

DevOps fosters a culture of consistent and optimal development, which inevitably results in improved applications and goods. Specifically, in software development, the idea is to reduce the amount of errors or bugs that occur in a product.

Higher customer satisfaction

There is a strong connection between customer service and satisfaction. The better and more optimistic the experience, the higher the satisfaction rating. This means, of course, that because DevOps improves CX, it also improves customer satisfaction, provided that the deployment is carried out properly.

Improved operational and process efficiency

As DevOps calls for the reassessment and evolution of current processes and development operations, there is a trend toward improved performance. As companies aim to enhance their entire operation, they are moving toward processes, methods, and practices that deliver improved performance. Common sense dictates that, overall, the whole company will see productivity gains as a result.

But there is also data to back up this move. A study by CA Technologies, *Accelerating Velocity and Customer Value with Agile and DevOps* (`https://docs.broadcom.com/doc/accelerating-velocity-and-customer-value-with-agile-and-devops-research-paper`), shows that organizations implementing DevOps see a 40% increase in the KPIs they monitor for organizational or process performance.

Transformation topologies

Every organization is different; even organizations in the same sector are different, for a variety of different reasons. To make transition as effective as possible, there are many different topologies for working with other teams in your organization, outlined as follows:

- Development and operations collaboration
- Shared operations
- DevOps as a service
- DevOps advocacy
- **Site reliability engineering** (**SRE**)
- Container driven

You will recognize some of these, possibly from your own organization. More do exist, though, and all of them are well documented with posters, available to purchase from *DevOps Topologies* (`https://web.devopstopologies.com/`).

> **Important note**
>
> It would be commonplace for you to start your transformation journey aligning to one of the preceding topologies and then switch to another model once you are mature enough. There is nothing wrong with this approach and in most scenarios this would lend itself to a higher level of success, rather than aiming for the top at the first attempt.

Development and operations collaboration

The first model is probably the most popular and is often seen as the golden model or the promised land of DevOps. This model enables smooth collaboration between the development and operations teams within your organization and is depicted in the following diagram:

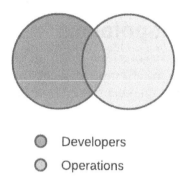

○ Developers

○ Operations

Figure 2.1 – Diagram showing collaboration between developers and operations

Each of the teams share knowledge where needed, but each of them will specialize in a specific product or part of the product. This will likely involve many different development teams.

This model is highly effective and works very well in organizations that have strong technical leadership. A word of caution, though—in order to achieve this model, you will need to go through a substantial level of organizational change.

In order to be successful, you will need a level of competence higher up in the management team. Also essential is that development and operations have very clearly expressed and demonstrably shared goals, be that improving reliability, increasing deployment frequency, or whatever your goal is.

Your operations teams must be comfortable working with the development teams and be familiar with some of their processes and tooling; this would include **test-driven development** (**TDD**) and Git for source control. Added to that, on the developer's side, they must take operational features very seriously and seek input from the operations team on implementations of the features.

Altogether, this needs a high level of cultural change from how those teams worked together in the past, so while highly effective, this is a difficult model to achieve. You may find yourself implementing a different model to start with and working toward this in the future as you mature.

Shared operations

If you work in an environment where you operate in product teams rather than individual functional teams, then we see the shared operations topology. In this topology, you see very little separation between the development and operations teams, and everyone is solely focused on a shared responsibility. The following diagram illustrates this:

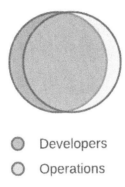

● Developers

○ Operations

Figure 2.2 – Diagram showing little separation between developers and operations

As with the previous model, this has the potential to be highly effective and will suit very well any organization that has a single product or service. Realistically, it's a form of the previous model we discussed but has some special features.

Organizations with a single product—such as Netflix, Spotify, Facebook, and Twitter—can achieve this topology. I would say, though, that outside of that single product focus, this topology is not very applicable.

In organizations where you have multiple product streams, the budget constraints—as well as the switching of focus between those product streams—will usually force your development and operations teams further apart, most likely back to the previous model.

Another way to describe this topology would be **NoOps**. There is no visibly distinct operations team in this model.

DevOps as a service

So far, we have looked at topologies that favor start-ups as they can build from the ground up in the right way, or enterprise organizations as they look to shift their operating model. For smaller organizations that may not have the budget, experience, or employees to lead operations aspects of the products they produce, the development teams may lean on an external service provider, as illustrated in the following diagram:

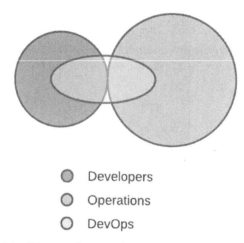

○ Developers

○ Operations

○ DevOps

Figure 2.3 – Diagram showing the DevOps as a service topology

The role of the service provider is to help them build out environments, provide automation of their infrastructure, and provide monitoring of the platform. The provider may also provide advice on the operational features needed in the development cycles.

Important note

Although we call the topology **DevOps as a service**, it's important to highlight that first, this model is not scalable, and customers must work the same way as the service provider for this to work well, which is not always possible.

This topology is useful for smaller organizations to learn about the operational aspects involved, such as automation, configuration management, and monitoring. This is where the issue lies for service providers trying to implement this topology as a business, as those smaller organizations are likely to move toward the first or second topology once their skills have built up, as they take on more operational staff.

Overall, this model has a chance to be somewhat effective with those smaller organizations with limited experience, but will likely stall if you try to implement it in larger organizations.

DevOps advocacy

When organizations tend to lean toward a large gap between development and operations, we can introduce an advocacy topology as a facilitation team. This topology can be used to help keep development and operations talking and collaborating, and is illustrated in the following diagram:

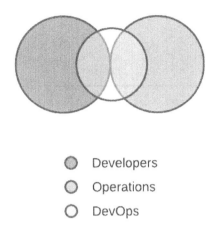

◉ Developers

◎ Operations

◯ DevOps

Figure 2.4 – Diagram showing the DevOps advocacy topology

This topology works well in all types of organizations, especially where that tendency for drifting applies. The results from this topology can be mixed, but you potentially can have extremely effective results.

> **Important note**
> When using the DevOps advocacy model, be aware of the DevOps team silo anti-pattern.

In order to be highly effective, the advocacy team must have the specific remit of facilitating communication and collaboration between the development and operations teams. Members of the team are often called **DevOps Advocates**, as their purpose is to help spread awareness of DevOps practices and facilitate bringing teams closer together.

A word of caution on this topology is that it can go wrong quickly. You must ensure that you keep your advocacy team separate from the day-to-day deliverables of the development and operations teams. They cannot get sucked into the work they do, otherwise they lose focus on their goal.

SRE

Often referred to as the **Google Model**, this topology is different from the others we have explored so far. DevOps will often say that development teams should join on-call rotations, but it's not a requirement. Organizations, including Google, run a slightly different model with a specific hand-off from development to teams that run the software. This is where SRE comes in, as illustrated in the following diagram:

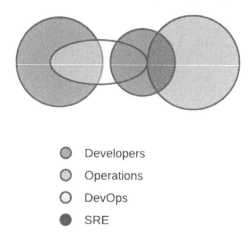

Figure 2.5 – Diagram showing the SRE topology

What is crucial with this topology, though, is the understanding that the SRE team has the final say on the deployment of code to production. The team can reject releases that do not meet the operational standards and ask developers to resolve issues.

Developers need to show the SRE team through logs, metrics, and test results that the release is of a high enough standard to be supported by the SRE team.

> **Important note**
>
> With the SRE topology, you need to be careful about the development versus operations silos. Simply renaming your team to *Site Reliability Engineers* and hoping it will work will fix nothing.

This topology is unique, in that while it sounds like a common model used in most organizations today, it will only really be suitable where a high degree of engineering and maturity exists. Otherwise, you will not fix anything and, without that level of maturity, the SRE team has no power to say no.

For this reason, this topology can either be very ineffective or highly effective—which way that turns out is entirely down to your culture.

Container driven

Finally, we have the container-driven collaboration topology. Containers can remove the need for some of the collaboration between development and operations. This is achieved by encapsulating the development and any runtime requirements of the application in a container. The container acts as a boundary between the development and operations responsibilities, as illustrated in the following diagram:

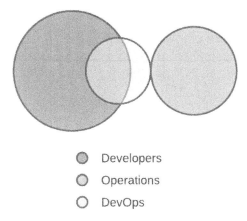

○ Developers
○ Operations
○ DevOps

Figure 2.6 – Diagram showing the container-driven topology

With a good engineering culture this topology works well, but if your developers start to ignore or not properly consider operational considerations, then this topology can revert to the usual *us and them*, just as with the SRE topology.

Just as with the SRE topology, be aware of the development versus operations anti-pattern, where operations are just expected to run anything the developers throw their way.

Transformation anti-patterns

In *Transformation topologies*, we explored the models that aid DevOps transformation and looked at what they set out to achieve. Here, though, we are looking at anti-patterns: these are ways of working that can be counterproductive to your goals and hinder your progress of DevOps transformation.

Each of the anti-patterns is specific, and I'm sure you will all have come across at least one of the following in your careers so far:

- Development and operations silos.
- DevOps team silo.
- Development does not need operations.

- DevOps as a tooling team.
- Glorified SysAdmin.
- Operations embedded in development.

Let's look at each of them in detail in the following sections.

Development and operations silos

This is one anti-pattern I know everyone will have experience of. This is the classic situation of *throw it over the wall* (or insert any other phrase you might use). In many ways, this anti-pattern, illustrated in the following diagram, throws up lots of questions:

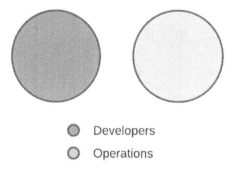

Figure 2.7 – Diagram showing the development and operations silos anti-pattern

From the developer's side, features can be marked as done and they can claim story points for them when their work is completed, but the feature may not be in production yet or may not even work in production.

The operability suffers as well because developers will not have enough context for features within operations, and the operations teams do not have the time or will to engage with the developers to fix the problems before going live.

Most of you will know that this is not the way we want to be working, but although we know this anti-pattern is bad and we know what the problems are, some topologies are, I think, worse.

DevOps team silo

The only situation I can think of where a separate DevOps team operating in a silo would be acceptable is where that team is around for a temporary purpose. This could line up to the advocacy topology we discussed in the previous section, whereby that team has a clear mandate to bring teams closer together and improve collaboration and communication between them, as illustrated in the following diagram:

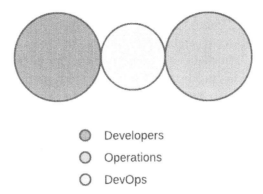

Developers

Operations

DevOps

Figure 2.8 – Diagram showing the DevOps team silo anti-pattern

This anti-pattern occurs when management or executives decide *they need to do DevOps* and start a *DevOps team*. This team will likely consist of people who are *DevOps engineers*; the problem is that this team will very quickly become their own silo. It will prevent developers and operations from becoming closer together, and tools and skills will become the subject of infighting, with everyone defending their corner.

Development does not need operations

When you mix the arrogance and naivety displayed by developers and their managers, specifically when starting new projects, often the assumption is made that operations is a thing of the past, especially when working with cloud-native technology. A wild underestimation is made about the sheer importance and complexity of good operational skills, as illustrated in the following diagram:

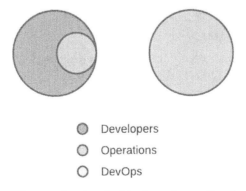

Developers

Operations

DevOps

Figure 2.9 – Diagram showing the "don't need operations" anti-pattern

The belief is that they can do operations without operations or use their spare time to cover the activities they perform. If teams recognize the importance of operations as a specialism that is as important and valuable as software development, then they would avoid lots of pain and basic operational mistakes.

DevOps as a tooling team

While the outcomes of this team can be beneficial, its impact is very limited. You can benefit from an improved toolchain, but the fundamental problem is a lack of early operational involvement and collaboration throughout the development life cycle, as illustrated in the following diagram:

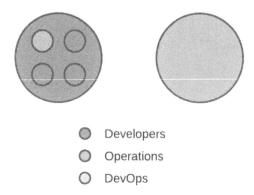

- ● Developers
- ◐ Operations
- ○ DevOps

Figure 2.10 – Diagram showing the DevOps as a tooling team anti-pattern

A DevOps team is set up to work on the tooling required for deployment, such as pipelines, configuration management, secrets management, and so on. This happens when you set up a team in order to not affect the current developer team's velocity (delivery of stories).

Operations teams continue to work in isolation and will continue to throw releases *over the wall*, just as with the first anti-pattern.

Glorified SysAdmin

The question of DevOps engineering has long been discussed. Many believe it's not a thing; I think it is, and it's widely adopted by many organizations. It's important to understand the differences between infrastructure engineers and DevOps engineers, though. I wrote a blog post on this very subject: `https://blog.m12d.com/hiring-the-ideal-devops-candidate`. This anti-pattern is illustrated in the following diagram:

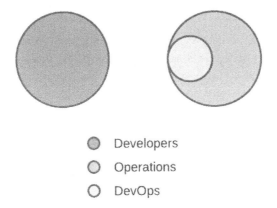

- ⬤ Developers
- ◎ Operations
- ◯ DevOps

Figure 2.11 – Diagram showing the glorified SysAdmin anti-pattern

This anti-pattern is very typical in organizations that have a low maturity in engineering. There is a strong desire to improve practices and reduce overheads, yet they will fail to recognize that IT is a core driver for the business.

Industry success with DevOps is not evident; sadly, this means some organizations want to *do DevOps* just because their competitors are. Instead of reflecting on the gaps in the current structure and relationships within the teams, the decision is made to hire *DevOps engineers* for their operations teams.

All this achieves is a rebranding of the previous infrastructure engineer role or SysAdmin role. There is no cultural or organizational change happening, other than the title often demanding a higher salary.

> **Important note**
> It's the human communication and soft skills that makes DevOps thrive, not the technical skills.

This anti-pattern is becoming more and more prevalent as people jump on the bandwagon, looking for candidates with tooling, automation, and cloud skills.

Operations embedded in development

When an organization—for whatever reason—does not want to maintain a separate operations team, development teams take responsibility for infrastructure. When this happens in product-driven environments, those items of operational responsibility are subject to resource constraints and often deprioritization, leading to suboptimal approaches, as illustrated in the following diagram:

⬤ Developers

◯ Operations

◯ DevOps

Figure 2.12 – Diagram showing the operations embedded in development anti-pattern

As with many of the anti-patterns we have discussed, this one also shows a lack of appreciation for the importance of effective operational skills. The value of operations is severely diminished, as it is treated as an annoyance for developers.

Avoiding failed transformation projects

The reality is that projects fail. DevOps transformation is no different and, as with all projects, you should be prepared for this and wherever possible learn from others' mistakes, putting controls in place so that you not only learn from those mistakes but also prevent them from happening again.

The top five reasons for DevOps transformation projects not going as planned and often getting abandoned are outlined here:

- Rooting DevOps initiatives within customer values

- Poor management of organizational change

- Failing to collaborate

- Failing to adopt an iterative approach

- Poor management of expectations in terms of DevOps initiatives

Let's understand these reasons better.

Rooting DevOps initiatives within customer values

Many companies across sectors are advised by the business side that they need to move faster to seek new opportunities and fight threats. You have this very real need for speed, but we have to make sure that we're grounding the need for speed in the value of the consumer. It's not enough that we need to get faster. We need to deliver value more quickly, or it may be that speed is not the concern; it is innovation that is required.

In conditions that cause confusion when attempting to solve a business problem, DevOps will help businesses experiment quicker to find the right answer.

Leaders who decide to do DevOps because of DevOps risk failure because workers do not have a connection to the word *DevOps*. Instead, you need to relate the benefit that these efforts offer to both workers and the company. This means knowing who the consumers are, what they consider to be important, and how to meet those needs.

Management of organizational change

One of the main issues, which I sadly see replicated over and over, is overlooking change in an organization.

When you try to incorporate something major all at once without learning time, this leads to low success-rate improvements. Leaders should initiate organizational change by recognizing and expressing the importance of the consumer. DevOps and the required improvements that come with it are not optional, and workers must understand that, along with why a change is needed.

We also need to concentrate on consumer satisfaction because customers are linked to value, not to the word *DevOps*. We need to iterate, to make sure that we have the ability to learn and develop.

Failing to collaborate

Effective DevOps projects require cooperation with all stakeholders to solve challenges that occur. However, many DevOps projects are limited to a single domain, which restricts their effectiveness.

> **Important note**
> Collaboration is a cornerstone of DevOps; failing to enable strong collaboration between teams will result in few changes to how you work, and may even make silos worse.

Organizations also often make the mistake of hiring workers on the basis of their technical abilities rather than their willingness to cooperate. When we put together a DevOps team, we want a team of people who work together—people who enjoy teamwork. They're smart, they're driven, they're skilled, they keep themselves and others accountable, and they enjoy learning, because DevOps is definitely not static.

We can still train good people on technical skills, but it's very hard to get people with poor attitudes and poor motivation to improve.

Failing to adopt an iterative approach

Launching DevOps in a single phase, giving training on Friday and starting the process on Monday, leads to higher failure rates, particularly for large organizations. A gradual, iterative approach lets companies concentrate on quality improvement and removes the danger of a quicker approach by allowing you a chance to learn, correct courses, improve every attempt, and step forward.

We need to create an environment where learning is at the front and middle, and iteration will help us do that.

The first-mover strategy is one of the better methods. *First mover* refers to a single-value stream with which businesses can be competitive by repetition and learning. The first movers should be politically friendly so that the stakeholders are willing to give DevOps a fair try, with the understanding that mistakes will happen and will be learned from, by creating an appropriate value to build credibility and increase support and presenting an acceptable level of risk to the company.

Our aim is not to incorporate the entire toolchain and an end-to-end, be-all and end-all, integrated solution from development to output. Our aim is to improve the workflow and keep improving over time.

Management of expectations in terms of DevOps initiatives

It's normal for stakeholders to get interested in DevOps' efforts to anticipate the wrong things. For example, many expect a workflow to minimize costs when it's really supposed to be a value game. Another false expectation is that DevOps is all about resources that can be applied easily, when it's really a hard lifting in terms of organizational change.

> **Important note**
> One of the single biggest things you can do to make DevOps transformation successful is set appropriate expectations. It always takes longer than you might think to transform to DevOps successfully.

At the end of the day, it all comes down to making sure that what you can deliver is up to standard. It's also one of the reasons why I'm going to warn people to be very vigilant about what they're committed to. Whether they're using numbers from consulting organizations or using numbers from market surveys, and so on, you really don't know what that's going to bring you in particular. But please be aware of your expectations.

Decoding failed DevOps transformation

Before we unravel the reasons behind the failure of DevOps, the crucial part is to understand what DevOps is. This is a point that we dealt with in *Chapter 1, Introducing DevOps and Agile*, but let's summarize those points once more, as follows:

- DevOps is more than team collaboration.
- DevOps is more than a toolchain.
- DevOps is more than a software development model.
- DevOps is more than agility and quality.
- DevOps is more than a bridge between development and operations.

Arguably, there is so much content about DevOps that it leads to confusion, and this causes issues during implementation for organizations. Some large organizations with the best tools struggle with DevOps because they do not get the basics right.

Culture has a huge impact on success

If you cast your mind back to *Chapter 1, Introducing DevOps and Agile*, I illustrated the importance of working on culture first before anything else. Culture is traditions, values, and beliefs that strengthen the organizational structure. DevOps is not just a collection of tools; you need to build a DevOps culture in your organization to get results.

Tools alone cannot help, so how do you set the right culture?

This follows on from the previous point, really. Organizations run after tools to achieve their aims, not cultural changes. This alone is one of the biggest causes of failure when it comes to DevOps.

The truth is that culture is tricky and difficult. We discuss this in greater detail in later chapters.

Defining DevOps for your organization

In this digital age, any organization is a technology-driven organization, regardless of the domain. The journey from *digital transformation* to *continuous digital journey* requires versatility, agility, and consistency as the most oriented aspects.

DevOps has become a necessity for companies concerned with software distribution or that also release upgrades or new functionality to serve their customers with consistency and supremacy.

Without a question, DevOps will make software development easier, but every company has a different set of requirements.

Automation and speed may not be what you think

Knight Capital, a real-time stock trading firm, used automation to make trades quicker and simpler for their customers. When writing new code for their application, the new code was mistakenly named the same as an old feature, which was inactive but was not removed from the application.

As a result, Knight's application made purchases worth billions in a matter of minutes, and the company had to pay a fine of **US Dollars** (**USD**) 640 million, which resulted in bankruptcy.

Often, organizations misinterpret automation. DevOps automates the software development process with the help of **continuous integration/continuous delivery (CI/CD)** principles. There are a huge number of tools available for source code management, testing, maintenance, and storage.

> **Important note**
> Automation is an incredibly powerful component, but you should never forget the power of the machine-man combination to improve accuracy.

DevOps means empowering everyone in the team

People are one of the key reasons for the failure of DevOps. It can't be all about growth and operating teams.

DevOps needs the participation of all the people on the team who consider teamwork to be a key function. To make DevOps effective, you need to find the right people, give them the right skills, and give them time to experience the DevOps culture.

A software engineer from a popular website was reorganizing database columns into a database-related tool in order to sharpen their own understanding. At the same time, they were not aware that they were also modifying column orders in the actual database. This resulted in the server being inaccessible to many users.

Summary

That concludes the second chapter. In this chapter, we looked at the key business benefits that DevOps brings to your organization, as well as looking at the topologies you can align your teams to for the greatest success. Flipping that around, we looked at anti-patterns, which are the team patterns to avoid when it comes to DevOps transformation. Finally, we looked at how to avoid failed DevOps transformation projects and looked at an example of how DevOps has failed.

In the next chapter, we look at how you can measure success within your organization and the importance of setting appropriate goals.

Questions

Let's now look back on this chapter and validate what we have learned. See if you can answer the following questions:

1. Which of these is not a key business benefit of DevOps?

    a) CX

    b) Boost in productivity

    c) Doing more with less resources

    d) Higher customer satisfaction

2. Which transformation topology is seen as the gold standard?

    a) Shared operations

    b) DevOps as a service

    c) Container driven

    d) Development and operations collaboration

3.   Which of these is a cause for a failed DevOps transformation?

   a) Failing to collaborate

   b) Adopting iterative approaches

   c) Cost savings

   d) Better employee retention

3

Measuring the Success of DevOps

You have to be able to point to metrics and measurements that show the success of DevOps within your organization. Selecting the right metrics is critical to showcasing your progress, ensuring teams stay aligned with the vision and empowerment of people. This chapter looks at the various metrics used in DevOps and how to measure success.

In this chapter, we're going to cover the following main topics:

- Common metrics used to measure success
- Designing metrics for your team
- Creating rollups at an organizational level

Common metrics used to measure success

Firstly, it's important to know why to measure your performance. I speak to many leaders of various businesses, and a frightening trend is that they all think measuring success is a tool that can be used to help with performance management.

The reality is that tracking of performance is a tool for improvement. **Continuous improvement (CI)** is a key pillar of DevOps, so if you have no idea how you are performing, how can you improve? Improvement should be the main goal of the metrics used in DevOps, ones that can drive tangible results and highlight growth areas.

Before we look at the metrics you can use, I like to put them into three buckets. Then, as you will see later in the chapter, depending on the type of team you are running, you can pick appropriate metrics from each bucket to look at your performance and generate useful methods of feedback. The number of metrics you pick from each bucket depends on your goals and your style of team. Have a look at the following diagram:

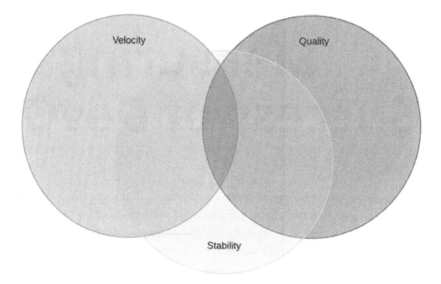

Figure 3.1 – Venn diagram showing the relationship of velocity, quality, and stability

The idea behind the preceding diagram is to illustrate that in an ideal world, you have a balance of metrics from each of the three categories, but you can have scenarios where you have more from one category. In all scenarios, you will notice that stability is present throughout.

The following possibilities exist in this model:

- **Velocity + Stability**
- **Quality + Stability**
- **Velocity + Quality + Stability**

Stability is core because whatever we are doing within our organization, no matter what changes we are going through, stability should be central to what we do, and in no circumstances should we impact this.

First, let's look at the metrics you would associate with velocity. In DevOps, when we talk about velocity, we mean working with both speed and direction.

Common velocity metrics

Velocity is vitally important in DevOps, as we are going on a journey that tries to break down silos in your organization and improve collaboration and communication. Having metrics that look at velocity can be very useful when it comes to highlighting areas for improvement. With that in mind, let's look at some of the common velocity metrics, as follows:

- Deployment duration
- Deployment frequency
- Change volume
- Test automation coverage
- Lead time
- Cycle time
- Deployment failure rate
- Environment provisioning time

From looking at these metrics at a high level, let's now look at them in more detail to understand what each one means.

Deployment duration

Deployment duration is the amount of time it takes to execute your **continuous deployment** (**CD**) pipeline. If you are producing a build and running a deployment at the same time rather than just picking up the latest build artifact, then record both the CI and CD pipelines, but make sure you have a way of knowing how long each pipeline is taking to execute. Most tooling provides you with the ability to look at the start and end time of each pipeline and the steps executed within.

Deployment frequency

Measuring deployment frequency enables you to look at how many times you deploy. In mature organizations, the target is to deploy numerous times a day. Whether you do or not is dependent on several factors.

> **Important note**
> Charting progress over time with an increasing number of deployments can show real progress in your DevOps transformation.

Change volume

In DevOps, there is often a common misconception that you don't follow the normal change management procedures. In reality, it's quite the opposite—transparency is important, and there is no better tool for transparency in service management than change management. You can measure the number of changes sprint to sprint, or even just monthly, to get an idea of the number of releases you are shipping.

Test automation coverage

Test automation is also a key part of automation in DevOps. When talking about measuring coverage in test automation, we mean the amount of the application or code base that is covered by automated tests.

Lead time

In DevOps, if you are looking to ship features quickly, then lead time is an important metric for you to measure. Lead time is the amount of elapsed time between adding an item to the backlog and that item shipping to release. This lets you measure how long it takes on average to take an item from backlog to production.

Cycle time

Very similar to lead time is cycle time. The slight difference in this metric is that rather than measuring from when an item is added to the backlog to when that item is shipped, cycle time looks at the time from when work on that item is started to when it is completed, or shipped.

Deployment failure rate

Identifying the rate of failure in deployment helps teams determine the quality of code and testing, moving from other stages to production. It is a leading indicator for code and pipeline maturity. Failure of deployments is obviously something you need to know about and monitoring can help with this, but recording your deployment failure rate as a percentage is also important. This lets you understand how often your deployments fail. Mature organizations look for a value below 5% for large volumes of deployments.

Environment provisioning time

When using **infrastructure as code** (**IaC**) to deploy your environments, much like when measuring deployment duration, environment provisioning time allows you to understand how long it takes to deploy your environment. In environments with a high number of microservices this is a great metric, as you will be able to see as you deploy more microservices how your provisioning time hopefully decreases.

> **Important note**
> As your organization progresses through maturity, it's useful to see where you have come from on your journey. Track this metric from the beginning so that you can see the progress you are making.

Now, let's look at some of the metrics associated with quality.

Common quality metrics

As we discussed earlier, measuring stability is important; second on that list is quality. You can have a high velocity, meaning you are working at a fast rate, but the quality may suffer because of that. This isn't a scenario you want, as low quality starts to erode trust in what you are doing and how you are doing it. Here are some common quality metrics you can use in your organization:

- Defect density
- Defect aging
- Code quality
- Unit test coverage
- Code vulnerabilities
- Standards violations
- Defect reintroduction rate

Now that we understand the quality metrics we can use, let's look at them again in more detail to understand what they mean.

Defect density

You can measure defect density in several different ways. The most common way is to calculate the number of defects per 1,000 lines of code. Using this metric is useful to help with sprint planning. You can, over time, use this metric to estimate the number of defects you may be presented with from sprint to sprint.

With the adoption of **integrated development environments** (IDEs) and automation tools it can be hard to identify lines of code, but it is still an important metric, and most development tools will be able to get past this limitation.

> **Important note**
> The calculation for defect density is defect count/**lines of code** (**LOC**) of the release. Note that this is on the specific release, not the overall code base.

Defect aging

This is a valuable metric to measure, and is simply the measure of time between a defect getting reported to the backlog and the current date, provided that defect is still open. Tracking this metric is important when it comes to technical debt. It allows you to understand how long on average you keep defects open for before they are resolved.

Code quality

When we talk about code quality, it's easy to think we are talking about the number of standards violations. We're going to talk about that metric as another quality metric you can use. In this context, when we talk about code quality, we mean in the overall context of an application. This can be represented as a percentage of the overall application. The degrading part of this metric is the number of violations against code quality, defined by many of the rulesets available for whichever language you are programming in.

Unit test coverage

Coverage of unit testing is measured as a percentage. It covers the percentage of the application that is covered by unit tests written by developers. In **test-driven deployment** (**TDD**) environments where the tests are written before the functional code, organizations look for 80% coverage as an absolute minimum.

Code vulnerabilities

Scanning your code for known vulnerabilities is a fundamental aspect of good security practice. For this reason, understanding the number of vulnerabilities by release is a key metric. You can introduce vulnerabilities in other areas of your application when you write new features or fix others. Tracking this metric then becomes important for ensuring you are following good security practices.

Standards violations

Static analysis tools can look at your source code in detail and highlight areas of code that do not conform to standards. These are generally community-driven or professionally set standards. However, some tools allow organizations to set their own rules for standards. This metric provides you with information and insights on how your developers are developing to standards baselines.

Defect reintroduction rate

Despite what you might think, this metric tracks the effectiveness of your developers' local testing. We are measuring with this metric the number of defects that are reported as breaking other functionality and causing other defects to be raised. You will sometimes see this metric being called *defect leakage*.

Finally, let's look at the common metrics for stability. You will recognize some of these if you have a service management background.

Common stability metrics

Stability is critical—just as poor quality can erode trust internally and within your customer base, so can poor stability. Nobody wants to use a product or platform that is not stable. Instrumentation is designed to help you understand what is happening and how it affects stability. The following metrics exist to help you measure stability:

- **Mean Time to Recovery (MTTR)**
- Deployment downtime
- Change failure rate
- Incidents per deployment
- Unapproved changes
- Number of hotfixes
- Platform availability

Let's now look at these common stability metrics in more detail.

MTTR

I find this metric powerful and more useful than measuring availability, especially in the cloud world, where availability of the platform is less within your control than within a traditional data center environment. Measuring MTTR looks at the time from when the system or product fails to when it is available again. Over time, this calculates an average that you want to see decreasing over time.

Deployment downtime

This interesting metric looks over time at the average time your application or product is unavailable during a deployment. You can measure this as a percentage of overall availability over the month or sprint, or measure the specific blocks of time.

Change failure rate

As we discussed earlier, it's important to make use of change management, own your failures, and measure the change failure rate as a percentage of changes implemented. This may be something the change management team already measures, but it is recommended to make specific measurement for your DevOps teams.

Incidents per deployment

There is no better metric to understand the impact releases make on your user community than by tracking the number of incidents raised per deployment. Systems such as ServiceNow have the ability to link in releases with incidents, so it's easy to see which release the incident is attributed to. This can go back in the backlog as a bug.

Unapproved changes

Any good change management function will track the number of unauthorized or unapproved changes on a platform. Some of them may be emergency releases and waiting for paperwork to catch up, but some of these may be genuine and represent learning opportunities.

Number of hotfixes

It is all well and good measuring the number of deployments you make and how quickly they happen, but what about the number of bug fixes or hotfixes you release? Looking to put measures in place to reduce this number is also a key differentiator between immature and mature DevOps organizations.

Platform availability

This is a typical metric that looks at measuring the time of availability of a platform, but representing this as a percentage. In its most basic form, the higher the percentage, the more available the platform was. Some organizations have credit schemes to compensate clients who do not get over a contractually agreed availability threshold.

That wraps up our look at the common metrics you can use to measure success in DevOps. But how do we apply these in meaningful scenarios, and what sort of baseline targets should you be looking at?

Designing metrics for your team

Now that we understand the key metrics that are involved in DevOps, it is next important to understand where those metrics can be used and in which scenarios. You can have too many metrics that you track in an organization, and these can then be counterproductive.

Knowing which metrics to use depends on many different parameters. However, we will now look at some example scenarios, describe what the goal of their DevOps transformation is, and look at the metrics that will help them identify their success.

Scenario 1: Small organization with a dedicated DevOps team

For small organizations, one thing that is common between them is their ability to become more agile and break down silos that exist between teams. Smaller teams allow for faster feedback loops and cycle time. In fact, most small organizations have fewer silos overall, and some may have no silos.

In this scenario, let's imagine we have a dedicated DevOps team at our organization, comprising six people. This organization runs one single product, which is sold to customers on a **software-as-a-service** (**SaaS**) basis.

In this example, the interaction is very simple. The team works well together due to the size of the organization, and roles and responsibilities are well defined. As with most organizations of this size, with the growth they have seen comes teething issues, such as a drop in quality due to pressure to execute.

For them, it's important to focus on stability as well as quality, to ensure that high quality leads to better stability. Let's now have a look at four metrics they could use and why, as follows:

- **MTTR**—Understanding how long it takes to recover the application platform is critical. The organization needs to look at how the platform needs to evolve in the future. This is important as the platform grows and scales, and information discovered here can lead to architectural improvements that reduce the average recovery time.

- **Platform availability** (> 99%)—Providing a contractual incentive to keep the platform available may help improve stability, but be warned: it could also cause unwanted pressure on the team and make the problem worse. Simple measurement and a discussion on what causes the downtime and how to fix it longer-term is much more productive.

- **Unit test coverage** (> 80%)—Ensuring good coverage of testing is very important. As this organization suffers from high levels of defects, ensuring good unit test coverage will ensure better testing is performed and that code is performing as expected.

- **Defect density** (< 1/1,000 lines)—Releases at this organization have presented problems before. Understanding the density of defects will help them plan better, as well as understand where the problems are when they are developing and which ones transpire into defects.

Let's now look at a different scenario for a medium-sized organization with an advocacy team.

Scenario 2: Medium organization with advocacy team

For this scenario, our organization has separate operations and development teams, and they're trying to work better together with the help of an advocacy team. Their aim is to facilitate the right level of collaboration and communication between them using different techniques, while still continuing with their day-to-day work.

As discussed in the previous chapter, advocacy teams are not given specific deliverable tasks in the sprint team, but are there to drive forward the best practices of DevOps and help the team achieve the goals set out for them.

For a team which is of a medium size, stability as well as quality is important to them on their journey, but understanding velocity is also important. The team needs a broad view of their performance over time so that adjustments can be made as they become more mature. Let's look at the metrics this team can use to track their performance, as follows:

- **Lead time**—Tracking lead time allows them to understand where time is used, from the allocation of a backlog item to when it is delivered. This helps the team plan better in the future, give appropriate estimates, and help identify areas where processes can be streamlined.

- **Cycle time**—Similarly, understanding the average time taken from work starting to shipping also gives the team metrics that help them improve their estimation and planning meetings, delivering over time to improve customer satisfaction.

- **Unit test coverage**—As a new team in DevOps, having high-quality code is important, but understanding where you are now is even more important. This helps highlight the amount of technical debt inherited by the lack of quality unit test coverage.

- **Code quality**—In a similar way to unit test coverage, this metric will help the team understand where skills gaps with their developers may exist and can be improved by targeting trouble areas.

- **MTTR**—Remember: stability is important, as is understanding how long it takes to recover service. This information for the team feeds back into their improvement cycles to again help them improve.

- **Deployment downtime**—Finally, any new team at DevOps needs to understand the impact of their work during releases. Measuring the downtime of your releases helps you improve the automation process in the future, or even move away from manual deployments to automated ones.

Let's now look at a large organization scenario where they have numerous DevOps teams.

Scenario 3: Large organization with numerous DevOps teams

When you have a large organization with numerous DevOps teams of various sizes, it's important to make sure each team focuses on their own priorities in terms of what their goals are. The overall goal of the business must remain in sight, though, and metrics can help ensure that the goal is tracked.

For this scenario, our large organization is looking to increase the pace of development and release across the board. Of course, as we discussed earlier in the chapter, this cannot be at the expense of stability.

Their challenge from a DevOps perspective is changing ways of working that have been carried out in a legacy fashion for a number of years, and some red tape exists that makes the process changes difficult and slow.

Let's now look at the metrics they can use to ensure the wider outcome of increased pace is achieved, while keeping an eye on stability, as follows:

- **Lead time**—Understanding how quickly things are dealt with from the backlog is important, especially in environments where teams are looking to pivot quickly and improve results. This can help you understand what you need to do in terms of making sure your processes are lean.

- **Deployment frequency**—Where the goal is to improve the release cadence, this metric is a must. You can understand how often you deploy, and do this in conjunction with other metrics here. Make sure that is not just a number but a number of quality releases.

- **Change failure rate**—Mistakes happen, especially in fast-moving environments. We can use this metric to help all teams understand if the releases they are doing are of high quality, not in terms of functionality but through adherence to the existing change management policies in place as they change the way they deploy.

- **Number of hotfixes**—It's OK to release hotfixes; they're a staple of the development life cycle. Tracking the number of hotfixes can help teams understand stability, but can also evaluate quality in parallel. It's a really useful metric to use in fast environments looking for quick change, but as discussed previously, mistakes can happen.

> **Important note**
>
> In these types of organizations, it can easily be the case that teams go their own way. Keeping them stitched together in terms of the overall goal is tricky, but finding common metrics can help explain that. Teams may have the same metrics, but leading and lagging indicators may be different based on products or acumen.

Let's now look at another small organization scenario, this time with an outsourced DevOps team.

Scenario 4: Small organization with outsourced DevOps team

For some smaller organizations who are looking to reap the benefits that the adoption of DevOps can bring them, outsourcing can be used to enable a specialist third-party team to work with the organization to achieve a number of goals.

This could be assistance with delivery, execution of agile methodologies, or support of environments and providing automation as part of the whole solution. Third parties can be used in numerous ways, and depending on the size of the organization and their requirements, this will change the scope of the third-party involvement.

For our small organization, a big focus for them is around the need to provide higher levels of automation, especially around testing. This will really help them drive forward where they are with DevOps.

Let's now look at the metrics we can use for this team, as follows:

- **Test automation coverage**—Due to the size of the team, they have outsourced test automation. Use this metric to look at the coverage of automation provided, and build up this number over time.

- **Deployment failure rate**—Deployment failure rates have many focuses, but this team has decided to look at failed testing gates. Using this metric will help the team understand what is failing, how often, and—through discovery—why it is happening.

- **Deployment downtime**—In a similar way to the preceding metric, tracking the amount of downtime in deployments can help with your third-party interactions. This can help you both work on and improve the CI and CD pipelines within your organization as you do more.

- **Platform availability**—Understanding how the third party is working within your environment is critical. Understanding platform availability is essential, and holding them to account when they make mistakes that cause outages is something you would need to consider. This needs to be handled properly, with no aggressive tones and an attitude of working together to improve things rather than penalizing.

In all four scenarios, you could use various different metrics to measure yourself; however, that doesn't mean that some metrics are worse than others. It comes down to what you are trying to measure, and you measure what you are trying to improve overall.

Now that we have looked at the various metrics you can use in different scenarios, what happens when you have multiple teams practicing, as in *Scenario 3*? How do you ensure that you report at an appropriate level? Let's look at the answers in the following section.

Creating rollups at an organizational level

Regardless of if you are practicing DevOps in your organization or not, clear communication is one of the keys to success. This is also true when it comes to communication of your **key performance indicators (KPIs)**.

You must ensure that the data you present back to leaders within your organization is clear, concise, and tells the appropriate picture about the performance within your organization.

In DevOps, especially when you are communicating organization-wide progress, you will first have to go on a journey of explaining what the metrics mean to the wider business. It's not immediately obvious what the metrics mean and show.

> **Important note**
>
> Try to display clear wording to executive leaders, even if this means changing the explanation of the metric. It's easier to relate it to something they understand than having to face questions on how it's measured, why you measure it, and more in executive meetings.

Another critical factor in DevOps, especially when measuring velocity, is to understand that not all teams are equal. Even from the inside, when it appears teams are delivering very similar things, the way they work and the way they operate as a team means the velocity of both teams is unlikely to be a comparable metric.

For this reason, I would *never* recommend comparing teams by using plain metrics such as velocity measured in **story points**. Teams can use this metric internally to see how effective they are at planning the work assigned to them and, throughout sprints, use the output from the previous sprint to see how they perform and where they can be better at planning.

> **Tip**
>
> If you are using story points to measure velocity of completed user stories, never make this metric public on executive dashboards.

Reporting when multiple teams work on one product

If your organization has multiple teams working on one product and each team is responsible for a different part of the product, then creating a rollup is quite simple. As with any project, you would report the overall progress against any plans. The same can be said in this scenario.

Each individual team may be working on individual features and requirements from different business analysts, but they will be working for—and aligned to—one common goal. For that reason, you need to understand what the end goal looks like, and from there you can create metrics that measure that goal.

This style is what might be known as an executive scorecard, or sometimes a business scorecard. It lists out the KPIs that show if you are on a path to success, or if blockers are in your way.

Reporting when multiple teams work on multiple products

When you have multiple teams working on multiple products, you can employ similar tactics to those outlined previously. Think of each product team as one, and create reports that reflect the work done by that team on that product.

Remember the previous discussion: no two teams are equal, and the same is said regardless of whether they are in the same product group or different product groups. Be careful not to compare teams across different products, even if they are working on the same deliverable, just in different products.

Depending on your organization, your multiple products may be completely unrelated, in which case it does not make any sense to create reporting that rolls up performance to a higher level.

If, for example, you are an organization that has products related to one another by a higher piece of marketing (maybe your organization has an overarching product that is actually made up of numerous products), then try where you can to align your reporting to that top level.

It is the top level that is understood across the business, so when it comes to reporting the velocity, quality, or stability metrics we discussed earlier in the chapter, make sure they relate to the highest level you can go that makes practical sense.

Creating goals that are S.M.A.R.T

Creating goals for your product or taking goals from an executive level and then disseminating them down to your team to be more actionable chunks of work can be a difficult task.

Within your department, you may need to break up a higher-level goal into more manageable goals between different teams. This is when the collaboration and communication with DevOps comes into its own. When one larger goal is split into numerous goals for smaller teams, working together and speaking to each other is critical in ensuring you achieve the fundamental task.

A common tool in the business world for setting measurable and achievable goals is using the **S.M.A.R.T** method. If this isn't something you have heard of before, this is what it stands for:

- **Specific**

- **Measurable**

- **Achievable**

- **Realistic**

- **Timely**

There are different versions of S.M.A.R.T. goals, but these are the definitions I prefer. It really means that to set a proper goal, it has to be something that answers the following five questions:

- What exactly do you want to do?

- How do you know when you have reached it?

- Is the goal within your power to achieve?

- Is it realistic that you can achieve this goal?

- When do you want to accomplish the goal?

I have used this method many different times before, you can find a lot more details about this method from *Mind Tools* (`https://www.mindtools.com/pages/article/smart-goals.htm`).

One easy example to follow is that you want to become trained in a specific tool—for example: *I want to understand how to create pipelines in Azure DevOps.* How would we now go about making this goal S.M.A.R.T.? Here's how:

- **Specific**—I want to learn how to create pipelines using **YAML Ain't Markup Language (YAML)** in Azure DevOps.

- **Measurable**—Ability to create working pipelines to deploy *Application X* without assistance from our **subject-matter experts (SMEs)**.

- **Achievable**—I need to learn how to build basic pipelines, then understand our own process so that I can learn appropriate items to add into the pipeline to complete the build.

- **Realistic**—By using online videos, working with our experts, and taking online courses I am able to achieve this goal.

- **Timely**—I will have achieved this in 6 months.

When you use the model shown here, you provide clarity toward the goals you are trying to achieve, how you plan to achieve them, what you need to achieve them, and—finally—when you will achieve them.

You may have multiple lines in a sheet describing your various goals, and you may use steps to describe the ways in which you will get there. The key is getting it down on paper.

Summary

In this chapter, we have looked at some of the most common metrics you can use to measure success in DevOps and looked at ensuring the importance of defining what success looks like. We have looked through some scenarios of different teams, highlighting the metrics that can be used to track their success. Finally, we looked at how to ensure you track at an organizational level rather than focusing too much on individual teams.

One of the biggest challenges in DevOps is measuring success. Using the skills you have learned in this chapter, you can implement meaningful goals and metrics to measure success in your organization.

In the next chapter, we explore how you build a culture within DevOps and how to break down silos in your organization for maximum efficiency.

Section 2: Developing and Building a Successful DevOps Culture

Culture is key to DevOps, and this section looks at how to build, foster, and develop a successful culture.

This part of the book comprises the following chapters:

- *Chapter 4, Building a DevOps Culture and Breaking Down Silos*
- *Chapter 5, Avoiding Cultural Anti-Patterns in DevOps*

4

Building a DevOps Culture and Breaking Down Silos

In this chapter, we will look at what culture means in DevOps, how you build a successful DevOps culture within an organization, and why culture is an important aspect of DevOps. We'll look at the characteristics of DevOps culture and how to maintain a strong culture within your organization, as well as how to break down existing silos in your organization.

In this chapter, we're going to cover the following topics:

- What is a DevOps culture?
- Why is culture important?
- Maintaining a strong culture
- Breaking down silos in your organization

What is a DevOps culture?

In previous chapters, we discussed a little bit about culture. Now, it's time to go into more detail. Culture has many meanings but for DevOps, when we talk about culture, we're really talking about a shared understanding between development and operations teams, as well as a shared responsibility for the applications they build. That then roughly translates to the following things:

- Increasing transparency
- Better communication
- Collaboration across teams

Despite what some people think, there is much more to DevOps than technology. DevOps is not a technological evolution of your tooling or the platforms that you use within your organization.

Culture in DevOps is also not letting teams define their own destiny; it is about working together. Implementing these things can be scary, but I want to take you through four things that can help practice this and build up the right culture in your organization.

All the things we are about to look at will help with the preceding key bullet points and start to foster the right culture in your organization.

Roles and responsibilities workshop

Defining very clear roles and responsibilities for your team helps create a strong culture. It prevents people from wondering what they should be doing and ensures that everyone knows not only what they are doing but how important everyone's role is to the overall team.

Include your team in this session; it's a very fulfilling experience and one that creates a mutual contract with your team, as everyone has participated in the development of the roles and responsibilities for the team.

Look at the following diagram. This is an example of what the output from a roles and responsibilities workshop looks like:

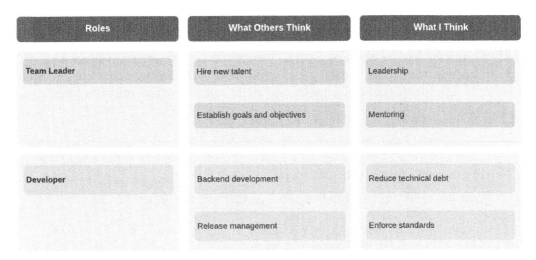

Figure 4.1 – Example roles and responsibilities matrix

You can use the preceding example to, with the help of your team, define the roles within your organization and then complete the responsibilities the rest of the team thinks that role should have.

> **Important note**
> If you are working remotely, convert this into a Word document and share it so it can be edited by the team collaboratively.

Once you have completed this step, work with the team to discuss what you have come up with and get an agreement of where the responsibilities lie. You may even find yourself moving them to another role, and that's OK, just as long as you make sure the team is in agreement.

Once the session is completed, make sure you share it with your team first, ensuring that no more feedback needs to happen. Once everyone is finished, inform other leaders that this is the way your team will be working.

This highly collaborative approach creates a strong relationship within the team, one that is difficult to break and will set you up for success.

Rules of engagement

It may sound like a term from the military, but this is a serious exercise and can prove valuable in the future. Think of the output of this exercise as a social contract with your team, one that should be refreshed on a quarterly basis.

Defining your rules of engagement defines *how you will work together*. If you are in a cross-functional team, then defining these rules early in the process can prevent tension from building up in the team. You could also call this a working agreement for your team.

Start by asking your team some simple questions:

- As a team, what is important to us?
- How can we avoid mistakes of the past?
- What do teams who work well together do that we can adopt?

Ask your team to write down their answers privately, to begin with. This moment of reflection for the team will help set the tone of the session. Next, ask the team to write down one statement that will make working together as a team successful.

When you are finished, collate all the answers together and combine any similar statements together. If you have a small team of fewer than five people, ask them to write down two statements.

Then you vote on the ideas as a team. The idea of the vote is a collaborative one, and the result is a commitment written down in the agreement. If an idea gets a vote of no, just ask what it would take to make it a yes and see whether the team agrees.

> **Important note**
> Follow up with your agreement regularly with the team; put it somewhere the team visits frequently so they are reminded of what you collectively agreed to.

The key is to facilitate an open discussion with the team that gets them thinking about how to work together successfully. Keep it open, honest, and, above all, respectful.

Retrospectives

Running retrospectives is something that if you practice agile you will be used to already. This technique focuses on getting the team together after each sprint and discussing the previous sprint in detail. Along with the **Scrum Master**, the team will look at the accomplishments of the last sprint as well as the things that did not go as planned and could be improved.

The atmosphere in retrospectives is one that fosters continuous improvement and learning. It is considered a safe space to discuss what is working, what may not be working, and what could be changed. Retrospectives are run after each sprint usually.

For larger organizations, you could run them by leaders from each of your teams monthly to discuss the adoption of DevOps. Much like sprint retrospectives, discuss with your leaders what is working, what is not working, and what they would change about your DevOps transformation.

The technique for running a retrospective is easy. A quick search will find numerous different ways of running a retrospective and from time to time, you should change how you run your retrospectives to keep the team engaged. I find them incredibly valuable to run as a leader and preparing for them takes no time at all. You should allow around 1 hour for your retrospective. You can even run them online very easily.

If you complete your retrospective in the office, then for your meeting space, ensure you get a whiteboard and some markers, as well as sticky notes and a timer displayed somewhere easily visible.

If you are running a remote retrospective, you can use software to have people place their virtual sticky notes on the appropriate heading. For in-person meetings, you can set up four different areas for people to place their sticky notes.

Now, for running a very simple retrospective, here is what you need to do with some appropriate timings:

- **Preparation (15 mins)**: Either digitally or on paper, set up four headings: *What Went Well*, *What Did Not Go Well*, *What Can We Do Better?*, and finally have one for *Actions*.

- **Ground rules (5 mins)**: Take no more than a few minutes to explain and set the ground rules. The key thing for every retrospective is to remember comments are not personal; every comment is valid, so listen with an open mind. Set the time period you will discuss (last sprint, month, quarter, and so on) and focus on improvement rather than pointing blame.

- **What went well (15 mins)**: Either write down and place upon the appropriate heading or create a digital card with your personal thoughts for what went well in the previous time period.

- **What did not go well (15 mins)**: Either write down and place upon the appropriate heading or create a digital card with your personal thoughts for what did not go well in the previous time period.

- **What can we do better? (15 mins)**: Either write down and place upon the appropriate heading or create a digital card with your personal thoughts for what you can do better compared to the previous time period.

- **Actions (10 mins)**: Finally, capture any actions from the retrospective. Ensure you take pictures of the outcomes or screenshots if you are working virtually. Discuss the ideas presented and assign responsibility for follow-up.

> **Important note**
>
> If you end up with a large amount of action, then use a voting system to enable yourself as a team to prioritize any immediate actions. Good examples of voting systems include Lean Coffee and Scrum poker.

Now that we understand what DevOps culture is, it's now necessary to understand why that culture is important.

Why is culture important?

I always like to describe culture as the backbone of DevOps. Think of DevOps like a tree where you have people, processes, and technology as branches, but they're all connected by culture.

In my various years working in and around DevOps with different organizations, all the work I have done has taught me that you can have the best processes in the world, the best engineers, and the best technology to support it, but if you don't have the best culture and do not look to improve on that culture, then it's all wasted effort.

Earlier in the chapter, we listed out the three important aspects of culture in DevOps; let's take a reminder of what those are:

- Increasing transparency

- Better communication

- Collaboration across teams

To understand why culture is important, let's take a look at these three areas in more detail. That way, we can build up a picture of why culture is so important.

Increasing transparency

Transparency is fundamental in many parts of business, but the further down the hierarchy you get, this can dilute, not on purpose but due to the way teams work and have worked historically. It is generally not the fault of specific individuals but rather a drift in culture from the organization as a whole.

Development teams are usually under a great deal of pressure to release software in their organization, which can lead to those teams going around the edges when it comes to controls put in place by operations. This single thing is what fundamentally leads to tension between teams as the developers now have infrastructure that is nonstandard and consumed in a way that operations cannot control. This all leads to what we call **shadow IT**.

You will find that many people point to public cloud services as a reason for this lack of transparency; however, this has been an issue long before the public cloud was even discussed. It is in fact the era of self-service that made this worse but even then, this has happened for a long time before either self-service or public cloud.

If you think of developers requesting virtual machines from the self-service portal, the operations team will deploy that infrastructure with the operating system only. At that point, their operations have no insight into that infrastructure anymore.

You can say the same about the public cloud as well, and this is what happens in many organizations when developers voice their displeasure about the performance of operations slowing down their work. They go to a public cloud provider and consume the services themselves.

What are the three main disadvantages of this approach, though?

- Verification of compliance with standards
- Infrastructure utilization and efficiency
- Cost control

Almost every organization I have spoken to at the start of their cloud journey has cited cost control as a problem. But what does this mean? Let's now look at some ways to improve transparency.

Verification of compliance with standards

With the delivery of a baseline operating system, or for cloud-native resources the baseline configuration of that resource, applications that are deployed and any database instances deployed on the virtual machines are all items that have standards in most organizations for compliance.

As an operations team, when you are blind to what is deployed on your servers and have limited control, you lose ground in your security posture and end up not knowing whether the applications and development tools are security patched.

The exact same scenario can be said when consumed directly from a cloud provider without the knowledge of the operations team.

Infrastructure utilization and efficiency

If your developers build 10 machines, with limited control, operations have no idea whether those resources are fully utilized, when they are utilized, whether they can be turned off outside of working hours, or whether they apply for a special licensing benefit.

These decisions, or lack of decisions, can have implications for capacity planning and the future ability to scale the platform and build critical services.

Cost control

Finally, developers are unlikely to realize the benefits of a cloud provider if they take that route on their own, the benefits of a scalable platform, and the benefits of overall spending a cloud platform can bring.

Spending outside of the main budget has an overall detrimental effect on the business and its ability to operate without distractions.

Better communication

Some of the things we have just discussed fall quite naturally into better communication as well. Imagine if developers and operations were able to communicate better with each other. From an infrastructure perspective, they could collaborate with operations to work on templates that match their requirements and operations could explain the controls in place for the security of the business.

That mutual understanding then becomes working practice and the developers get the infrastructure builds in a timely manner and operations keep control.

This isn't the only place where better communication helps you build culture though. Communication can be made more efficient in a number of different ways:

- Operations participation in sprint planning
- Developers performing releases
- Operations working in development sprints
- Developers working in operations

These examples may seem trivial, but they can have a real impact on the overall experience of those involved and can make them think about their interactions. Over time, this helps improve communication.

Operations participating in sprint planning

One of the classic pieces of feedback you will hear from operations teams is that developers rarely develop for the environment and that operational challenges, concerns, and requests are not taken into account.

One of the models we discussed in the *Transformation topologies* section in *Chapter 2, Business Benefits, Team Topologies, and Pitfalls of DevOps*, talks about bringing operations and developers closer together. In *Chapter 1, Introducing DevOps and Agile*, we also discussed how agile plays a part in DevOps. When you start to move toward agile working, getting closer to one of the transformation topologies we explored, you will start to have operation teams working more closely with developers anyway.

> **Important note**
> When operations participate in planning and before work on the sprint starts, they have a chance to voice any concerns about things the developers may not have considered that are in their field of expertise.

Starting this process early can have real benefits. At the beginning, it will be tricky, and it may feel unnatural for people who have not worked this way before, but persevere with it and the results will be clear.

Completely changing the way people work presents them with challenges and you will come up against resistance.

Developers performing releases

For many organizations, it is the developers who take the compiled applications and release them to the production environment. Try having your developers work with operations to specifically perform releases.

> **Important note**
> We want conversations between operations and development to be authentic and transparent. If both teams are notified of this change in the process in advance, it can lead to prepared statements and assumptions. Bring the operations team into a normal stand-up and allow this feedback to happen in real time.

The benefit of doing this is that your developers should start to understand and have an appreciation of the work that needs to be done with every release of the application.

Operations working in development sprints

In a similar fashion to previously, flip that around and have your operations teams do some work during the sprints with developers. Not only will they gain an appreciation and understanding of the development process, but you will also find that they can contribute during the sprint on operational matters.

> **Important note**
> Doing this can mean that operational issues are resolved during the development sprint and before release, rather than an issue coming up after release and causing more tension between teams.

The majority of the time, you will find that operations teams cannot write software, so bring some of the operational tasks you would normally perform into the sprint, not only will you get better at communication, but you will start collaborating as well.

Developers working in operations

Just as mentioned before, flip that idea on its head and have developers working with operations. This will give the developers an understanding of how important it is to understand the operational elements.

This working model can increase collaboration as well as communication and give a mutual understanding. Now developers understand what happens during an outage, how monitoring works, and how instrumentation in the application affects the operational processes, which will make a difference in how the application is developed, for the better.

Collaboration across teams

What exactly do we mean when we say collaboration? In the context of DevOps, it is working and creating together. Collaboration is essential for any business but when your teams are both diverse and global in presence, this is even more important.

From a technology perspective, you'll find no shortage of tools to enable your teams to collaborate more. But when we talk about collaboration, how do we define it, and how can we improve it?

> **Important note**
> Collaboration tools can help, but they're not the whole solution. Choose a collaboration tooling that fits your needs the best.

The primary goal of collaboration within DevOps is to reduce any operational delays that exist as well as communication gaps with teams that are geographically dispersed. This is the part of DevOps that requires the cultural step change so many people talk about.

Your teams need both shared goal definitions and a single-team approach to their work. Identify a common set of goals, which lays the foundation for the future working relationship. Managers and leaders should also create a culture of inspiration, honesty, trust, and respect in their teams. This makes everyone feel like a part of the team and creates a stronger bond and message of what you are trying to achieve.

A clear roadmap is also critical that defines your path to success and helps in achieving the goals you have set out to do. The roadmap should be crystal clear with the avoidance of any ambiguity. Regular check-ins and discussions with your teams also help provide clarity as you progress.

One final point here is about diversity, which is key. A close-knit team requires you to get to know everyone and how they work, and even understanding their culture and personal situations. In remote teams, when people work in different time zones and have different cultures and religions, this is incredibly important.

Now we understand in detail why culture in DevOps is important for our organization. Let's look at how you maintain that culture and develop it.

Maintaining a strong culture

Now that you have spent time building up the culture in your organization, the last thing you want to do is see all that effort go to waste. It's important to maintain the culture you have built up so far, so it continues to foster the good practices you have put in place already. In fact, a survey by DZone (`https://dzone.com/articles/top-10-barriers-to-devops`) found that 14% of people said culture was a barrier to DevOps adoption.

As with most things, though, the daily running of a team and business can provide a number of threats to how strong you can maintain culture. Some things can even have a negative effect. Some of these might include the following:

- Starters and leavers
- Pushing too hard for success
- Lack of innovation
- Cultural differences
- Lack of buy-in

How can we avoid these roadblocks to our culture? Let's have a look at each of them.

Starters and leavers

In any organization, people leave and people start. This is one of the most common elements of any business. Hopefully, the culture you have created means that when people leave, they are leaving for better opportunities that your business cannot provide, rather than leaving because of acrimonious reasons.

Knowing how to deal with starters and leavers in high-performing agile teams is something that agile leaders have to deal with all the time. It's important that you start off any new member of staff the way you mean to go on.

This starts with making sure you bring the right people on board, which is easier said than done. As you already have an open culture with the team, seek out thoughts from the team about what a new member of staff should bring to the team. Be prepared to listen in a collaborative way, but also be prepared with your own ideas so you can counter if you feel the need.

> **Important note**
>
> When it comes to the interview process, include members of the team to validate your thinking on the individual's attributes and what they can bring to the business.

When it comes to leavers, following the practices you have in place should ensure that when a member of the team leaves, they don't leave a large hole in the way you work. Of course, people often become good friends with their colleagues and someone leaving can have an emotional impact on a team more than anything else.

Watch out, though, as this emotional impact can start to affect productivity and quality. The longer a team has worked together, the better rhythm they have together and when that is broken, it can have an effect on the team.

Replace the member of the team as soon as you possibly can to reduce any impact. Someone new in the team can often bring new ideas to everyone and give the team a renewed energy.

When you have a significant change, run the roles and responsibilities exercise at the top of the chapter. Before the member of staff leaves, run a retrospective. If you think about it, that person leaving is a key moment and one that can be time-boxed. Learn from a wider perspective what worked, what did not work, and what could be improved.

Pushing too hard for success

When you have put lots of effort into building a culture and seen positive results, you can get into a mindset that makes you push too hard for more success. This can be as a team or as an individual. Either one of these will have a detrimental effect on what you have done so far and will be something you need to monitor closely.

The simple reason to watch out for this is that when you start to push for success, you can slip back into old ways and cut corners to get more success. Stick to your guns, though, and don't overcommit work you cannot deliver and keep producing the strong results you have got used to at this point.

> **Important note**
>
> Following the processes of continuous feedback and continuous improvement will yield more success as you progress. Let it come naturally and don't force the issue.

If you do that, you will find that success comes naturally to you and you don't need to push yourself or your team for more success.

Lack of innovation

One attribute of high-performing teams is their ability to innovate. Teams that are used to having the ability to innovate will continue to crave innovation. The ability to experiment and innovate is critical to the success of any business.

Watch out for the pace of innovation slowing down, or worse, other teams putting barriers up to your team innovating. This should be considered a red flag and one that makes you focus as a team to resolve the issues preventing you from innovating.

Try not to get too distracted by this and deal with the situation as a leader, letting your team continue as normal. Do not, though, engage with the team and tell them they're no longer able to innovate.

Many DevOps professionals set themselves apart from others due to their ability to innovate quickly and come up with new ideas. Telling them they cannot do something that is within their domain of expertise is going to be damaging to the overall team and the culture you have built up.

Cultural differences

We have already talked a couple of times about remote teams, especially ones that are geographically dispersed. We discussed earlier as well about diversity and the important role that it plays.

Cultural differences also refer to those of the teams you work with. Everyone has an understanding of how things may be done within the organization. The problem, as we discussed, when looking at anti-patterns is that they may not line up with what you want to do as a team. The whole reason for this is why DevOps now exists.

You can combat cultural differences in the team objectives by aligning goals. The key here is to keep doing this time and time again to make sure teams are tightly aligned. When team goals start to diverge is when they start to operate in old ways again.

Lack of buy-in

Apart from the lack of innovation, one of the biggest impediments to maintaining culture is still the lack of buy-in. You may be thinking that to get to this point you have done the hard work and executives are already bought in. Of course, you are right, but just like in your own team, executives change, priorities of the business change, and the business trading environment can change.

This is a common situation, and you need to make sure leaders are still bought into what you are doing, the reasons why you are doing it, and the results you have achieved so far to get you there.

> **Important note**
> When it comes to buy-in, don't be complacent. Leaders change, and with this change can come new ideas on how things should be done.

To combat this, keep a note of the successes you have had as a team and make sure you can replay your journey along DevOps to show how that success has come about.

As you can see, it takes effort to not only build the culture but maintain it as well. Make sure you visit some of the tips and exercises shared in this section to keep the culture in your teams strong. Now, let's look at how to break down the silos that exist within your organization.

Breaking down silos in your organization

In DevOps, culture is brought about by the need to break down silos in your organization between certain teams. Silo mentality is behavior-driven and can be resolved using a number of techniques. A silo exists when teams operate independently and often have a crossover of their activities or lack of consideration for others' work.

The danger of silos in the business world is that trust is destroyed, communication is cut off, and complacency starts to set into what you do day to day. Teams that are siloed cannot react to change quickly or take advantage of opportunities that present themselves.

Worst of all is transparency, when data cannot be shared between teams freely, which impacts your ability to make data-driven decisions about your team or business. Some of the things we are about to discuss we have touched upon before:

- Creating one vision for team collaboration
- Working toward common goals with collaboration tools
- Educating together, working together, and training together
- Communicating often
- Evaluating team compensation

Let's look at each of these in a little more detail.

Creating one vision for team collaboration

We talked earlier about the importance of creating common goals for your teams and how they should also share one vision. It is counterproductive to have a vision for one team that is completely separate from another if they do no move toward a greater result.

All teams should share, buy into, and adopt that one vision. When goals that conflict with other teams are set, silo mentality begins, meaning silos are often created by management.

The leadership team must understand the long-term goals, departmental objectives, and key initiatives of the organization, before passing the unified vision down to the teams. The unified leadership team will, thanks to this approach, encourage trust, create a sense of empowerment, and break managers out of the *my department* mentality and into the *our organization* mentality.

Working toward common goals with collaboration tools

The biggest downside to the silo mentality is that people see things from their perspective. This, of course, is not always a bad thing, but when this happens, people will make choices toward their own team, rather than from the company perspective.

One of the simplest ways to keep everyone on point with common goals is to use a dashboard to highlight progress toward your common goals. This is a form of collaboration.

When organizations give their employees quality tools for collaboration, people will naturally share more information and because of that communicate better with each other.

Finally, when the entire organization looks to understand each department (sometimes each team) and the specific issues they face on a day-to-day basis, departmental goals can become the goals of the entire company.

Educating together, working together, and training together

From experience, one of the easiest ways to break down silo thinking is to perform cross-organization exercises and events. Training on this level can really help start breaking down silos as they get to know other people in the organization.

Working together can also have a big impact. Consider the idea of sitting people closer to each other if feasible. When people work close to others, they build rapport; as problems in their work arise, they look to those close by for answers. This can have a big impact.

Specific training is also a key way to make sure that you can shift the silo mindset from your organization. This training involves supporting the ideas of collaboration, teamwork, and communication.

Communicating often

I firmly believe you cannot over-communicate. Regardless of the situation, frequency of communication is very important. When you communicate often, this introduces a level of trust and transparency.

When teams feel this level of trust and transparency, data flows between teams and facilitates the breaking down of silos rather than breaking them down by one action of communication.

Organizational structure is a silo and some organizations try and remove this structure to remove silos. This will not always work though. It's more effective to communicate properly in this situation than to remove that organizational structure, which is important to the delegation of duties.

Evaluating team compensation

Competition between teams can be very healthy, but compensation plans between teams can create silos and an unhealthy relationship where competition becomes the goal rather than working together.

If you have bonus or compensation plans within your business, make sure that they reflect the goals you set as an organization and do not play teams off against each other and what they are setting out to do.

When compensation plans align with the company goals, employees are driven to collaborate, communicate, and achieve goals together.

Summary

In this chapter, we have looked at DevOps culture and understood why culture is important in DevOps. We have discussed the need for increased transparency and better communication and the need to maintain a strong culture. Finally, we discussed the need to break down silos in your organization and the importance of this in DevOps.

In the next chapter, we'll explore anti-patterns in DevOps and discuss how to avoid them.

Questions

Let's now recap some of what we have learned throughout this chapter:

1. What are the key pillars of culture?

    a) Roles and responsibilities, rules of engagement, and retrospectives

    b) Teamwork and collaboration

    c) Great social life with colleagues and retrospectives

    d) Completing work as quickly as possible and pushing other teams hard

2. How can you promote better communication in your organization?

    a) Have developers take time off.

    b) Take everyone on team-building courses.

    c) Have developers perform releases.

    d) Let your operations team block all releases.

5
Avoiding Cultural Anti-Patterns in DevOps

Following on from learning about the specific challenges of breaking down silos between teams and understanding the importance of culture in DevOps, in this chapter, we will look at the challenges of building culture in DevOps – specifically, the anti-patterns that can be blockers to culture. This is not an easy task and requires careful planning and thought.

In this chapter, we're going to cover the following main topics:

- Organizational alignment
- Resistance to change
- Difficulty scaling up
- Excessively focusing on tooling
- Legacy infrastructure and systems

Organizational alignment

Alignment across the organization is critical. Later in this chapter, we will talk about resistance to change, and when we should instigate change for the sake of it, without a clear vision or goals. This will create a high level of resistance in the organization. Alignment helps reduce resistance.

> **Important Note**
> Increased competitive advantage, increased revenue, increased profits, and reduced costs are just some of the things to expect with better organizational alignment.

Success with organizational alignment starts with answering the *what*, *why*, and *how*. Putting the appropriate measures in place at each step is what helps generate better alignment:

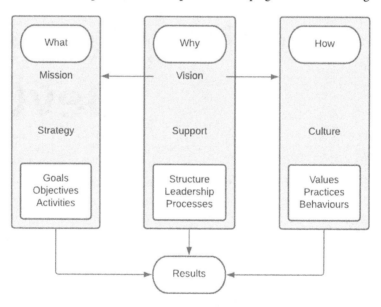

Figure 5.1 – Organizational alignment to generate results

Achieving alignment is fundamentally based on the three pillars of **what**, **why**, and **how**. The *what* phase revolves around making sure the mission statement is well defined. The strategy is also something that should be defined here as well. This is done by defining goals, objectives, and activities. A company mission statement is an example of defining **what**.

Next, there's the *why*. Define your vision and the support structures that help the organization get there. Organizational structure is important here, as is the role of leadership and the processes that are used to help us achieve *why*. An example of this could be "*Our vision is to create better everyday lives for many people.*" This could be the vision statement for a medical organization.

In terms of *how*, this is the culture of the organization. Culture is made up of defining values, the practices within the business, and the behaviors we expect within our business.

Putting all these together is what generates results. Vision also drives *what* and *how*. This concept is something that is explained very well by Simon Sinek in his session *Start with Why* (`https://www.ted.com/talks/simon_sinek_how_great_leaders_inspire_action`).

That concludes our look at the effects of misalignment and how it can derail your DevOps transformation. Now, let's have a look at what resistance to change means for your organization.

Resistance to change

Change happens – it is a frequent occurrence in any business. Sometimes, these changes are forced, while other times, they happen because of the need to change for the good of the business. Regardless of the scenario, in most organizations, we will likely come across resistance to change. If that resistance is not handled properly, our DevOps transformation can go off the rails before it's even begun.

Therefore, it is critical to perform a DevOps transformation to understand how to deal with organizational change, understand the roles involved, and the steps needed to make it successful.

Understanding the roles of organizational change

When navigating through DevOps transformation, for employees, this is a major change to the organization. When we are making any major change to how the organization operates, it is important to understand the roles of the two key players that make this happen successfully. These roles are management and **human resources (HR)**.

Management

Leadership is critical in this situation. To avoid scenarios where employees become so dissatisfied with how changes are being handled that they leave, leadership and the executive team need to have unilateral support for the changes that are proposed.

Conversations between managers and their teams, starting from a one-on-one basis, will help unify the team toward committing these changes. These conversations are crucial. It should be an open environment where we discuss how the changes affect them and what they think about the proposed changes.

As managers, we should be asking the **why**, **what**, and **how** questions. Unfortunately, though, many managers are not well versed in organizational change management. This lack of skills can make it difficult to implement the changes required.

To increase skills in this area, HR should provide appropriate training for managers, which will be useful for situations like this but also serve as good knowledge as managers further their careers up the management chain.

Human resources

In any organization, HR provides a pivotal role in implementing changes of any size. HR can provide communication, implementation, and tracking for any changes. The real value of HR comes with their ability to speak impartially with concerned employees about these changes, why the business is making them, and why employees are important to this change.

> **Important Note**
> Whatever we do, we must make sure we engage HR in conversations from the beginning. They can only help when they understand the proposals, why we are proposing change, and how it will benefit the business.

HR can help increase the buy-in of organizational change by championing the change and providing employees with the support that's needed across the various impacted teams. SHRM has two great resources that are worth looking at regarding this subject.

The first one is *What is HR's role in Managing Change?* (`https://www.shrm.org/ hr-today/trends-and-forecasting/special-reports-and-expert- views/pages/deb-cohen.aspx`), followed by *HR Can Improve Employee Buy-In for Organizational Change* (`https://www.shrm.org/ResourcesAndTools/ hr-topics/organizational-and-employee-development/Pages/ ImproveBuyIn.aspx`).

Organizational change process steps

When going through organizational change, to be successful, we should follow a methodical process. It's important to make sure we work with all the stakeholders from top to bottom in our organization to, well, ensure success.

Let's have a look at the six key steps to achieving success in organizational change.

Clearly defining the change and aligning it with business goals

This may seem obvious, but many organizations don't do this well. It is one thing to articulate the change we are making, but it is another thing entirely to compare this against your organizational goals and performance objectives. This step is important because the right changes aligned with your business goals will move the business in the right direction. After all, that is why we are making the change in the first place.

The other benefit to this step is that it allows us to evaluate the change we are proposing against the value it will bring. Why change if it doesn't bring sufficient value?

We should be asking the following key questions at this stage to ensure we are getting the most value:

- Why is the change needed?
- What do we need to change?

Let's learn how to determine the impact of change across the organization.

Determining impact across the organization

When we have determined the change we want to make and know it has real value, we should assess our organization and determine the impact it will have.

It is important to understand that change does not just affect one business unit within your organization – change reverberates around the business and has a cascade effect for everyone. The information that's gathered here will be valuable in figuring out where training is needed and where employees need support.

Some of the key questions that you should be answering at this stage are as follows:

- How will change be received by employees?
- What are the impacts of the change?
- Who will the change affect the most?

Now, let's learn how to develop strong communication strategies to deliver our message of change.

Developing a strong communication strategy

It is key that everyone is part of the transformation journey. The first two steps will have told us about the employees that are directly affected and obviously must be included in any communication. However, transparency is key, so communicating with the whole business should be a focus of your communication strategy.

Your strategy for communication should include a timeline on activities, the communication channels we want to use, the mediums we want to use to present the information, and how it will be communicated incrementally.

We should be asking two key questions at this stage of our transformation:

- How will we manage feedback?

- How will change be communicated?

Training is a part of change that is often missed. Now, let's look at how to provide effective training.

Providing effective training

Now that our transformation message is out in the open and we understand the gaps in the organization, our employees need to know how training will be delivered and what training we will be providing.

This is important because employees will want to know what skills they need in order to perform the roles under the proposed changes. Training could be provided in the form of online learning modules, classroom-led training, shadowing with subject matter experts, or mentoring.

To provide effective training, ask the following questions:

- Which training methods will be the most effective?

- What skills and behaviors are required to be successful?

Supporting employees through change is critical. Let's look at how we can provide support structures to employees.

Implementing an effective support structure

When going through any organizational change, it is important to develop a support structure for employees. Change can be unsettling for employees, so having an effective support structure can help overcome this.

Effective support structures in organizational change will assist employees both emotionally and practically as the skills and behaviors needed for the role change. Mentorship, as well as having an open-door policy with leadership, is the critical thinking that's needed to allow employees to ask questions as they arise.

Some of the key questions you should ask when implementing an effective support structure are as follows:

- What types of support will be the most effective?
- What support is required the most?

Finally, let's look at how to measure the progress of change in our organization.

Measuring the progress

Finally, let's look at measurement. Throughout the process of organizational change, a structure should be put in place to measure the impact of the changes we are making throughout the business. This measurement step allows for continuous feedback and improvement along the way.

This is also an opportunity to evaluate your change plan, determine how effective it is at what we are setting out to achieve, and document any lessons we are learning. We can also use this, if required, as an opportunity to tweak and change the plan. There is nothing worse than continuing with a flawed plan that will not lead to success. Don't be afraid to change as we go, should that tweak lead to success.

The key questions we should be asking at this stage of the process are as follows:

- Was the process successful?
- Did the change assist in achieving our business goals?
- What could we have done differently?

Now that we understand the steps of organizational change, let's look at how to overcome resistance to change.

Overcoming resistance

We have already discussed some steps we should be using during the change process. A lot of these things will help us overcome some of the resistance that we are facing.

These won't help everyone, though, and communication, as we've mentioned previously, is crucial for getting this right. Constant communication to help with aligning our goals will help put people at ease. Resistance comes when people feel threatened or worried about changes that may occur.

Some of the main reasons for resistance to change within an organization could be as follows:

- Fear of losing your job
- Poor communication
- Lack of trust
- Fear of the unknown
- Poor timing

Now, let's look at these reasons in more detail.

Fear of losing your job

In every business, to stay competitive and to stay relevant with your customers, change is required. Sometimes, companies will need to add new roles, downsize, or even change roles to achieve these goals. For most people, this is where the fear of losing their job comes in.

Poor communication

I'm losing track of the number of times we say communication is important, but it really is, as it will make or break a transformational change. Communication solves all ills in a change, but lack of communication creates many.

Employees need to clearly understand why change is needed and what it will help the business achieve. If employees are thrown the idea that "*everything they've been doing is wrong and it's going to completely change*," expect a huge backlash.

Lack of trust

Successful businesses are built upon trust. If the level of trust between leadership and employees on the ground is high, then your resistance is going to be low. However, in organizations with mutual distrust between leadership and employees, the business is not heading in the right direction, so successfully implementing your change will be very difficult.

Fear of the unknown

There is a saying in business: "*there are unknown unknowns.*" When people don't know what is happening, that generates fear, which leads to resistance. This can easily be fixed with good communication. The more we communicate, the more open we are with our communication, which breaks down the fear of the unknown and builds trust. These two things alone will reduce the amount of resistance in your organization.

Poor timing

From experience, how and when the message of change is delivered is one of the key problems. It's usually not the act of change that creates resistance with employees, but how and when that change is communicated.

Breakdown in communication

Communication is key, period. In my opinion, we cannot overcommunicate anything in business. When communication breaks down, it has a severe impact on business. This manifests itself in causing frustration in terms of money and time.

Breakdowns happen when the communicator does not efficiently communicate what they are trying to say. This could be through spoken works, how those words are understood, or even written words. There is not just one way to break down communication. It could be the communicator who misspeaks or the recipient who does not interpret the communicator correctly.

Business can take a lot from the aviation industry, where communication is of utmost importance. Failure to communicate clearly between pilots and air traffic control can result in huge losses of life. Throughout the history of aviation, the industry has learned from their mistakes and made the skies safer. We should do the same.

Avoiding communication breakdowns in your business comes down to five key things. Let's have a look at them:

- Owning mistakes
- Slowing down
- People coming together
- Winning people
- Patience

Let's look at each of these in detail.

Owning mistakes

Humans have a fear of making mistakes, which can come from the fear of disappointing, previous mistakes that have been made, or other reasons. Owning your mistakes is important because shifting the blame to an innocent party is just going to make things worse.

If we've misunderstood someone, we should just let them know. This helps correct the problem before it really becomes a problem. The communicator will then understand what went wrong and can improve their communication strategy next time.

Slowing down

Pace is important, so don't rush things. We can make breakdowns worse by rushing into resolutions. Shift the pace to moving more slowly; if we rush into things, people think it's not important, or that we want it out the way. When we slow down, that changes as we are taking the time to think about it, so it's important to solve.

People coming together

Above all, make sure your strategy is around bringing people together and not pushing them apart. Communication breakdowns divide people and destroy trust. Getting everyone on the same page – in the same room, if possible – and focused on the same goal starts to bring people closer together.

Winning people

Usually, when communication breaks down, some key people are responsible for that. Clearly, it should be around fixing the problem instead of playing a blame game. As we discussed earlier, blame just creates problems with trust.

Patience

Frustrating is a word we might use to describe communication breakdowns and getting out of them is quite difficult as well. We need to be patient, though: a lack of patience will only make things difficult.

A lack of patience is often part of the cause of a communication breakdown and will only be remedied by acknowledging and enforcing it culturally. Sadly, resistance to change is all too common, but we can get through it! Now, let's move on and look at the difficulties of scaling up our DevOps transformation.

Difficulty scaling up

One of the other anti-patterns in DevOps comes with the ability to scale up what we are doing. Most businesses will encounter issues in scaling up when they start out. With growth, especially rapid growth, comes challenges in scaling up your business.

Scaling your business is difficult. Many changes are needed and can derail even the most successful business. Some challenges we can expect with scaling up are as follows:

- Having to scale before market fit
- Working with the wrong people
- Focusing too much on sales and marketing

- Price competition

- Management structure as growth occurs

- Ignoring issues

- Forgetting making yourself lean is part of scaling

All these challenges list are really from a business perspective, but what about scaling DevOps specifically? When it comes to scaling up, we need to stick to specific steps and focus on growing certain aspects of our DevOps practices:

- Start with small teams

- Encouraging skill development

- Prioritizing culture

- Continuous feedback

- Automation

Let's have a look at these five areas in a little more detail to get an understanding of what we need to do.

Start with small teams

Have you ever heard of the "*innovator's dilemma*"? It speaks to the challenges of innovating in your business when we are in a cycle of reality or our day-to-day operations. If we wish to scale, removing this impediment is fundamental to our success.

We must decide on what we want to deliver, create an agile team to work on advocacy, and help scale our operations and remove blockers. We must acquire the skills we want in this team and work toward a logical resolution before moving the team into other teams.

Encouraging skill development

This is where we introduce the growth mindset, or the learner's mindset. We must be willing to try something new and work with different teams. The mindset of the employees in these teams is crucial in starting out on the right foot.

To get the best from both your developers and operations teams, encourage them to grow their skillsets – not just from a technology perspective, but also soft skills as well, which are equally important in DevOps.

Prioritizing culture

Success in DevOps comes with developers and operations having a positive culture between both teams. It's easy to think that DevOps is all about developing products, but it is important to develop the right relationships. Culture is as important as other aspects of DevOps.

The hard part is getting everyone onboard. Therefore, small teams are fundamental to starting this. Getting these things right will enable your teams to take on more as they develop. Teams that follow the early adopters will learn from them also.

Continuous feedback

Continuous feedback is a very important step in adapting your DevOps culture based on what is happening and how people are performing. The process of getting feedback enables us to understand what is happening with our product and what needs to change to make it better.

Wherever possible, if we can, separate release from deployment. We can work toward iterated deployment, thereby getting feedback from our user base and incorporating those changes into future releases.

Automation

Maturing your automation capabilities will help you scale. When it comes to automation, find what hurts in your processes and look to automate this. However, don't focus too much on this; otherwise, we'll experience some of the things we will discuss in the *Excessively focusing on tooling* section.

If we want to achieve continuous delivery, then we really need to be looking at automating our testing. Without automated testing in place, we are going to find it hard to perform continuous delivery.

So far, we have looked at organizational reasons for anti-patterns in DevOps. Now, let's look at the effects of focusing too much on tooling.

Excessively focusing on tooling

So far, I have touched on the importance of the other aspects of DevOps before focusing on tooling. The dangers of putting too much focus on tooling are evident from numerous studies we can find online.

However, the reality is that we can focus on tooling too much compared to culture, people, and processes. Even after this point, you can excessively focus on tooling. This can damage your transformation efforts.

One of the most common areas of technology in DevOps is around automation. This could be automating your CI/CD pipelines or other processes, be it technical or business. From my experience, though, many organizations take the message of automation in DevOps to an extreme – one that is counterproductive and sometimes harmful to businesses. That begs the question, how much automation is too much? Let's have a look.

How much automation is too much?

It is important to understand how organizations get to this point. Let's imagine that most organizations are moving from a traditional waterfall methodology to an agile methodology, which is new to them. It's common to see organizations take agile to the extreme, which comes from overusing agile and, in turn, DevOps.

> **Important Note**
> The key question should be, does automation serve the *what* and *why*?

Research from *451 Research* (`https://www.scriptrock.com/automation-enterprise-devops-doing-it-wrong`) shows a trend that backs this up:

> *"I think there is a tendency to think that large enterprise organizations, with all their divisions and teams and silos, are capable of doing what Facebook or Netflix have done with their cutting-edge implementations of configuration management tools. All of the legacy technologies and processes have to be considered as well."*
>
> *– Jay Lyman, 451 Research*

The toolchain is full of examples of organizations promising to make your organization the next Spotify or Netflix. While that is an admirable place to get to, fundamentally, your organization is neither Spotify nor Netflix and never will be.

When we try and replicate the successes of these organizations from any perspective, but especially technology, we will quickly find ourselves on a downward path. Any investment we have made will, at this point, be worthless as we have tried to automate too much and push too much tooling.

Striking a balance

It is important to know and understand when to automate or implement a tool to achieve a specific thing. In fact, some organizations I have worked with in the past do no automation in DevOps; some do CI/CD automation, while others automate business processes.

Automation is about taking a manual process and placing technology around parts of or the whole of a process so that this can be replicated through automation. The problem is that not all processes can or should be automated. Note that different parts of a process can be automated; it's not always about automating either the whole process or no part of the process.

When we're deciding whether something should be automated, we should take a step back and follow a simple process. Let's put this into the context of software development processes:

1. Think about the processes that take place during development with the rest of team, vet them, and lock them.

2. Decide on the tooling for automation.

3. Look at the value of automation, step by step.

> **Important Note**
> If your processes are flawed to begin with, adding automation to them just makes a bad process happen faster and without oversight.

Your organization is also unique, and vendors have a habit of pulling us in with fancy marketing and telling us what they're doing with different software vendors. However, our organization has been selling books for 100 years. We're not a unicorn start-up and mixing old and new systems is going to be a challenge.

Breaking down processes

When it comes to our software development processes, we can start to break them down further. We can do this with any process – I'm just using software development as our working example.

During this process, we break down our components into sub-processes. These are our candidates for automation. When we have sub-processes, we are in a perfect place to look at them in detail. At this point, can decide on whether we should keep, fix, or create new processes.

It is important to take your time. Creating processes may seem trivial, but think about how the business wants to operate in the future and how it operates now. Processes must have the ability to grow with the organization through changes.

DevOps-related enabler tasks such as CI, CD, or continuous testing should also be combined with any fixed processes at this point.

Finally, you must select your tooling. This is where most organizations fall off the rails and things go wrong. When we have defined our processes and figured out which DevOps components will be integrated into them, we need to work on the right tooling for the job.

Organizations that over-automate will typically focus on the actual tools rather than the process itself. Technology in this scenario is often based on emotions, such as other organizations using similar tools or their colleagues from a conference using them.

This situation just ends up in mass confusion for everyone involved. The result is too many tools and processes being used that must be adjusted for the tooling, when in fact your tooling should be adjusted for the processes.

When automation causes problems

I want to talk about an example I have come across. I worked with an organization that wanted to go from nothing to completely automating the life cycle. That way, developers could do everything end to end, at any time of the day. The grand vision was to enable the build anywhere, anytime scenario.

However, the reality was that developers would release new code to the platform twice a day, sometimes more. The result of this behavior was that end users just became frustrated with the constant changes.

For me, the nail in the coffin for this experiment was that the automated testing was not holistic. Quality issues that could have easily been resolved by humans doing some of the performance and regression testing slipped through the net.

In the end, the organization removed some of the tools from the toolchain, limited the types of changes that could be made by the developers, and put more rigor around the review process, deployments, and, most importantly, testing.

The moral of the story here is to not let grand plans and visions, along with the insatiable need to automate, overrule the part of us that applies rationale to how and why we automate.

Do no harm

I hope that, after reading the preceding sections, you are not put off by agile or DevOps. That certainly wasn't the intention. The fact remains that the value we can get from DevOps will far outweigh the cons of DevOps, but we must be smart and methodical about our implementation.

Overall, technology is an enabler, and when used properly, it's something that adds a tremendous amount of value to your organization and can make the work we are doing much easier and more repeatable.

The gold nirvana that is DevOps is something that comes over time through how we need to perform agile and the core DevOps principles in our organization, rather than how others do it. Many organizations can end up using tools to satisfy the vision of someone else rather than their own.

In this section, we have looked at the effects of having an excessive focus on tooling. Now, let's move on and look at what legacy infrastructure and systems mean for DevOps.

Legacy infrastructure and systems

Of course, DevOps is not just for the cloud; it can be for hybrid environments and, of course, on-premises. DevOps is arguably easier with cloud environments, but legacy infrastructure, systems, and thinking can be real blockers to DevOps.

Legacy infrastructure causes several issues when it comes to DevOps adoption since these systems are not designed for the continuous processes that come with DevOps. Releasing in iterations with legacy infrastructure is also very difficult and, in some cases, impossible. This breaks the whole DevOps ethos and starts to introduce challenges we need to overcome.

Legacy modernization

One of the ways we deal with technical debt from legacy infrastructure is to go through a modernization process. This represents a journey from traditional infrastructure to more modern services, for the most part in a public cloud provider.

Modernization has many benefits for businesses looking to scale as it helps reduce costs, improve customer experience, makes the time to market faster, and enables agility in the business, among other things.

One of the most common routes to modernization is to move away from existing monolithic applications to a **microservice**-based architecture and design patterns. This pattern represents a domain-based architecture where services are decoupled from one another and can be reused for multiple purposes.

Legacy applications and infrastructure present several challenges to us:

- Security
- Single point of failure
- Lack of flexibility

The move toward more modern application principles and practices helps solve and address concerns in these areas. When it comes to processes and people, this is where DevOps can help. These are, of course, non-technical areas. These areas are as important as the technical areas when it comes to solving your legacy infrastructure concerns.

Summary

In this chapter, we explored the anti-patterns associated with culture in DevOps, looked at the challenges this brings to our DevOps transformation, and how to resolve some of these issues to prevent them from overburdening our efforts. Finally, we looked at the effects excessive tooling has on our environment and the dangers this brings to our efforts.

In the next chapter, we'll look at value stream maps and learn how to use them to drive process change. We'll also look at the difference between value stream mapping and process maps.

Questions

Now, let's recap what we have learned in this chapter:

1. Which of these is not a reason for resistance to change?

    a. Poor timing

    b. Poor communication

    c. Concerns about pay rises

    d. Ownership of mistakes

2. Which of these can be done to improve breakdowns in communication?

    a. Owning mistakes

    b. Take everyone on team building courses

    c. Continuous feedback

    d. Bringing people together

Section 3: Driving Change and Maturing Your Processes

Processes make your organization tick and are a key aspect of efficient working. Understanding how to mature them is key.

This part of the book comprises the following chapters:

- *Chapter 6, Driving Process Change with Value Stream Maps*
- *Chapter 7, Delivering Process Change in Your Organization*
- *Chapter 8, Continuous Improvement of Processes*

6
Driving Process Change with Value Stream Maps

To fully understand processes, we must know who executes the process, when it is going to be executed, and why it is going to be executed. This information can help in breaking down processes and eliminating redundancies so that useful processes can be automated.

This chapter will help you improve the process flow within your organization by reducing unnecessary processes using **value stream mapping**.

In this chapter, we're going to cover the following main topics:

- Understanding value stream mapping

- How does value stream mapping help?

- Differences between process maps and value stream maps

- Explaining an example value stream map

Understanding value stream mapping

The process of value stream mapping comes from value stream management. In turn, value stream management is a lean business practice that aims to understand the value of software development, delivery, and resources.

This process can also help the flow of value within an organization, while also providing life cycle management for software delivery. With value stream mapping, instead of teams focusing on features, this can help your teams focus on what works and start to shift away from things that do not work.

So far, we have looked heavily at the cultural aspects of DevOps and what it means for your organization with respect to their transformational journey toward DevOps best practices. This chapter will start to focus on the processes within your organization. Processes that are lean are processes that work well, contain very little waste, and are highly efficient. Once you have achieved this level of efficacy with your processes, you can start to automate.

> **Important note**
> Automating bad processes implies that you make bad processes happen faster. Apply lean practices to them first, such as value stream mapping, to make them as efficient as possible.

Going through a value stream mapping exercise offers a plain and simple view of your processes from the perspective of customer experience. The result of this is better alignment with business objectives and the ability to scale agile and DevOps transformation.

The first step in this process is about changing your mindset, so that you look at software development as a direct link to business goals. We've spoken about the changes that are required several times already. The same can be said when we're trying to make our processes lean.

Activities you perform in software development and business goals are often given a wide berth from each other, and the different priorities of software teams keep them caught up in those priorities. In this scenario, where nobody is aligned, you must take a step back to see if you are in alignment.

So, the first logical step is to take a pause and back up a little. Evaluate what is happening in the business, and then look at how the work you are doing in software development is helping and supporting the business in achieving its goals.

During this process, evaluate where you are with the people, processes, tools involved, and any dependencies that exist so that leadership has complete visibility into how things are going.

Going beyond DevOps for process improvement

It is true that DevOps has accounted for a huge amount of organizational change and transformation within the software industry. This has evolved over time, from the initial focus on teamwork and empathy, to how we can drive real value to the organization.

As we have discussed already, to get the best return on investment, you must focus on the business value you are generating and the customer satisfaction that comes with this. This was something we discussed in *Chapter 2, Business Benefits, Team Topologies, and Pitfalls of DevOps*.

For many organizations, they would agree that DevOps has provided a large amount of transformation. However, you will still find a number of enterprises that fail to understand and explain the value that is achieved from the investment required.

As your practice matures, you need to focus more on understanding and creating metrics and KPIs to measure success. These metrics should increase the quality of any software you deliver further and speed up delivery to satisfy customer experience, as well as show the business value you are delivering.

The key message here is that successfully implementing DevOps will help a tremendous amount, but you must go much further in your level of process maturity.

Taking a look at value stream mapping diagrams

The following diagram is from an article on value stream mapping from Plutora (https://www.plutora.com/blog/value-stream-mapping):

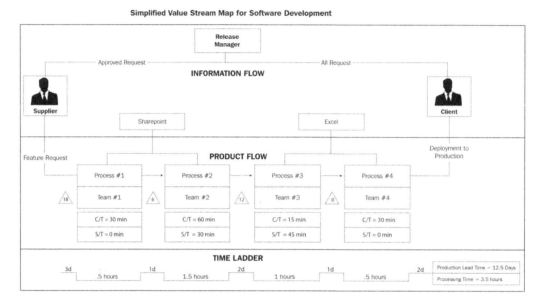

Figure 6.1 – Example diagram from a value stream mapping exercise

We will look at the preceding diagram in more detail later in this chapter. The previous example is some output from a value stream mapping exercise.

The value stream map is a diagram that is split into three primary areas. These areas are information flow, product flow, and time ladder.

Information flow

This section of the diagram shows how any information related to the process communicates, as well as how data is transmitted. The diagram shows the release manager taking in all customer requests. Only approved requests are submitted to the development queue, which is shown as a supplier.

Depending on the goal of the value stream mapping exercise, the collection and distribution processes shown in SharePoint and Excel can include numerous levels of detail, as well as a number of other integrated systems.

Product flow

This section looks to map the steps of the software development life cycle all the way from the initial concept through to delivery. Depending on your requirements, you can focus on specific parts of the process if you are looking to gain efficiencies at specific points. It can be as detailed or as high level as needed.

The task that is being performed is shown in the box, as is the individual or team performing the task in the box. Key process data is then shown below this. The example in the preceding diagram shows two items. C/T refers to cycle time, while S/T refers to setup time.

You can include any number of details at this point that highlight any important information you wish to show. Triangles show the queue of features that are waiting at each stage of the process, followed by dotted arrows from one stage to another. These are called **push arrows**. These show that the product is being moved from one stage to another, as opposed to being pulled.

Time ladder

The purpose of the time ladder is to provide a really high-level or simplistic view of the timeline involved in the value stream. The top portion of the ladder represents the average amount of time that your feature will spend in a queue, gate, or waiting at each stage in the process.

The bottom portion of the ladder shows the average amount of time where active work is engaged. More specifically, it shows you when value has been added to the feature during that specific stage.

Other terminology

Let's look at some of the other terminology you may come across in value stream mapping diagrams:

- **Cycle time**: This refers to the frequency of features that are produced, or the average time between two completed features.

- **Setup time**: This refers to the amount of time needed to prepare for any given step. In software engineering, this could be the time needed to understand requirements.

- **Uptime**: This is measured as a percentage and provides you with the total time that any processes or systems are active.

- **Lead time**: This measures the average time needed for one request to make its way through the entire cycle from concept to delivery. We discussed this in *Chapter 3, Measuring the Success of DevOps*.

- **Takt time**: This is the rate you need in order to produce features to meet customer demand. It's a calculation that takes the number of hours in a working day, multiplied by the number of working days in a month, divided by the number of work hours available, converted into minutes per month. Based on 9,000 minutes in a month and 150 features from your customers, dividing those means you have 60 minutes or less to complete each of those features to keep up with the volume.

Let's now look at the symbols used in value stream diagrams.

Value stream symbols

You will notice some specific symbols in *Figure 6.1*. Much like a flowchart, these represent specific things. Let's look at the symbols you can use within your value stream diagram:

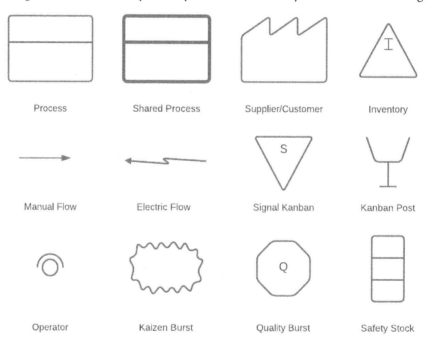

Figure 6.2 – Symbols used in value stream diagrams

Of course, many more exist, but the ones included in the diagram are common, and you will certainly need to use them in your own value stream maps. You can also group them into categories. The top row includes all the material flow symbols, the second row includes information flow symbols, and the bottom row includes a general set.

Now, let's discuss the key terms involved in material flow, information flow, and process flow diagrams in detail.

Material flow

The following terminology is commonly used in material flow diagrams:

- **Process**: Represents a single individual or team performing a specific task.
- **Shared Process**: The same as a regular process, but the process is shared between numerous parties.
- **Supplier/Customer**: Generally, when this is in the upper left of a value stream, this is the starting place of the flow and indicates a supplier. When it's in the upper right, it represents the customer.
- **Inventory**: Use this if you want to add an inventory count between two processes. As in our example, we put the number of features outstanding at that point in time.

Information flow

The following terminology is commonly used in information flow diagrams:

- **Manual flow**: Indicates where conversations or notes are passed and the type of information that's flowing.
- **Electronic flow**: The same as a manual flow, but it represents an electronic information asset.
- **Signal Kanban**: This is used when the inventory drops to a minimum and signals the production of several parts. Think supermarket stock levels.
- **Kanban Post**: Typically, this indicates a location for collecting signals. It can also be used to exchange withdrawal and production in Kanban.

General

You may also need to use the following in your diagrams:

- **Operator**: This shows how many operators are needed to process the value stream map at a specific step.
- **Kaizen Burst**: Sometimes called a **Kaizen Blitz**, this is a burst of team activity focused on resolving specific challenges. Its purpose is to resolve the challenge and focus the team on a problem.

- **Quality Burst**: This indicates a problem in quality and can be used at any point in the value stream mapping chain.

- **Safety Stock**: This indicates a temporary safety stock to prevent problems, should a failure occur, or if other issues are present.

Now that we understand some of the fundamentals of value stream mapping, let's look at how value stream mapping can help within your organization. Some of the terminology we've used so far has been a little generic, so let's make examples more specific to software engineering.

How does value stream mapping help?

Value stream mapping is incredibly important. Not only does it help you understand your processes, but it also helps translate that understanding into methods that improve your processes. It is critical to business sustainability.

There are three reasons for this:

- Eliminating waste improves the bottom line for your organization. You also discover the root cause and source of waste using this process.

- Teams will discard individual assumptions and prioritize them based on the perspective of the customer.

- Wasteful handoffs can be identified easily through visualizations that have been created with value stream mapping. Teams can identify and react to improve their collaboration, communication, and culture.

While the process of creating value stream maps can be incredibly useful to your organization, it can also present some challenges. Let's look at these challenges in more detail.

Challenges of value stream mapping

Value stream mapping can be a wasteful exercise if you are not careful about how you execute it. You need to be aware of common pitfalls that exist, including creating value stream maps and making sure that what you produce is itself of value to your business.

Return on investment is crucial when it comes to value stream mapping. Monitor the level of effort you need to invest to conduct a value stream map for a process and balance that against any potential value you get from it. Keep an eye on your return on investment from the start.

The process of identifying waste can be intensive. It's common to come across fear and uncertainty when employees know value stream mapping is occurring. They wrongly assume this process is used to identify waste from an employee perspective.

Many processes involve cross-functional teams and several other complexities. You should make sure you involve people that are experienced from all sides of the process when conducting value stream maps.

While baby steps are a fantastic place to start making savings by improving steps here and there, these step improvements may not impact the overall bottom line until top-to-bottom changes are completed.

> **Important Note**
> Remember, the goal of value stream mapping is to cut waste, not create any more than what you already have.

We discussed the symbols you can use in value stream mapping exercises earlier in this chapter. My advice would be not to rush to professional solutions to create them. Start off by using paper or a whiteboard; the results are the same and you can outline your idea. You can formalize the value stream map later using software to achieve this.

Use cases of value stream mapping

Based on the descriptions of some of the symbols we looked at earlier in this chapter, you will hopefully have guessed that, like many lean processes that come from manufacturing, value stream mapping has its roots not in software engineering, nor in technology, but in manufacturing.

Value stream mapping can bring value to several industries. The principals apply equally to each of them, and you can adapt to your needs like in any framework. Fundamentally, the industry or domain that you are operating on determines the items that flow through the value stream map.

For example, when it comes to supply chains, value stream mapping is essential to finding and eliminating costly delays, which leads up to the finished product. In the services industry, the process will facilitate timely services for customers, as well as effective services.

In healthcare, value stream mapping will ensure that patients receive high-quality care while reducing any delays that could be life-threatening. Finally, in manufacturing, value stream mapping helps identify waste by analyzing each step of both the material and information flows. Process items, which flow through the value stream, are called materials.

Identifying and reducing waste

As we mentioned in the previous section, value stream mapping originated in manufacturing, just like the lean principals themselves. Lean has its origins in the automotive industry in Japan. This enabled the Japanese car industry to flourish through lean principles and automation while the rest of the world was still catching up.

Applying that lean thinking to your day-to-day processes is harder than you might think. In the manufacturing industry, the following eight things are wastes:

- Defects
- Overproduction
- Waiting
- Non-utilized talent
- Transport
- Inventory
- Motion
- Extra-processing

When applying lean thinking, try thinking about the eight things in the preceding list to see where you can make improvements to your processes. Let's run through some examples in software development that can help you identify waste.

Transport

In manufacturing, we think of transport as something physical: moving from one place to another. Transport is probably one of the hardest types of waste you can discover in software development. After all, the product is not something physical that you move – it is something virtual.

Instead of thinking physically, think about how your tasks are going from one developer to the next. This could be from an architect to a developer, or a designer to a developer.

A practical example of this could be developer to tester. Let's assume that your tester is ready to work on your task and they've just finished working on another, so that it can be worked on immediately. First, the tester will look at the task to understand what they need to do. Next, you must start the application and get to the step you want them to test. It can take time for them to get to that point. This is what is called setup time and, in this example, that time is generated by the handover.

Waiting

Waste in terms of waiting can be found with **work in progress** (**WIP**), as well as waiting for the next step in the process. If you are waiting, then that work is not getting processed efficiently. Tasks that wait on someone or something else provide non-value-added time. This delays delivery, not just of that item but all items.

Good examples of this in the software engineering area would be quality control steps such as testing, as well as technical debt and bug fixes.

Overproduction

In software development, this comes in two clear forms. The first will be very familiar to you, and this is scope creep. To clarify, scope creep is when you start off with an initial set of requirements, but after you start working on those requirements, they change.

The second type of overproduction comes into play along with the **Pareto principle**. The application of this principle is that 80% of your target audience will only use around 20% of your features. Therefore, this principle dictates you will spend a large amount of time developing features that will hardly be used.

Now that we understand why value stream mapping is so important and understand how to identify waste, let's have a look at the differences between process maps and value stream mapping.

Analyzing differences between process maps and value stream maps

Value stream mapping shows a significant amount of information and uses a more linear format. It is very different from a process map, which only shows the steps involved in the process. The same differences also apply to flowcharts, as shown in the following diagram:

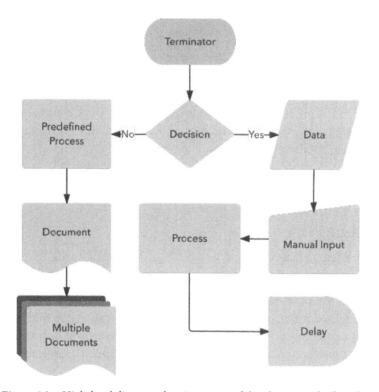

Figure 6.3 – High-level diagram showing some of the elements of a flowchart

As you can see, a flowchart or process map does a great job of showing the parts of the process, including the points of decision throughout the process. However, it does not go that step further as a value stream map does.

Value stream mapping attempts to identify waste within processes and between process steps. Process mapping, on the other hand, forms a more detailed picture of the business process.

Take the following example diagram from *Creately* (`https://creately.com/blog/diagrams/process-mapping-guide/`). The following process map diagram clearly shows the different parts of the process:

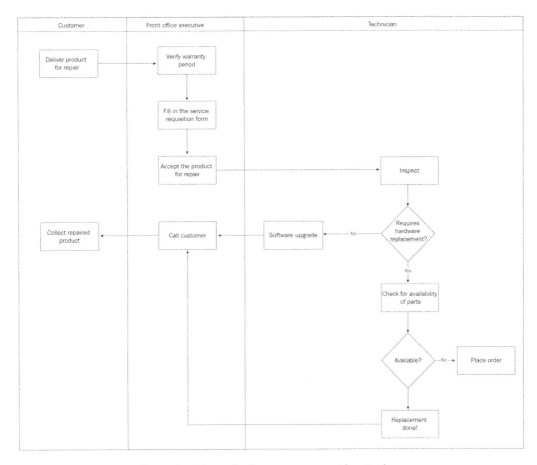

Figure 6.4 – Example of a process map with swim lanes

The preceding diagram shows what are known as swim lanes. These are the vertical columns you can see. In the previous example, they separate parts of the process into different people who interact with the process. You have the customer, front office, and technician in the preceding diagram.

This is useful for highlighting who deals with the parts of the process you are documenting; it can move in and out of different swim lanes, and the number of swim lanes you have on a diagram is entirely dependent on the process.

The following diagram, also from *Creately*, is a simpler example of a process map. It's simply read from left to right, following the arrows:

Figure 6.5 – Simple example of a process map

The regular boxes are steps in the process where something happens, while the rounded pill shapes are initiators and terminators – in other words, where you start and stop the process.

When to use either a process map or a value stream map is clearly something critical that you need to understand. You can spend lots of time creating both process maps and value stream maps and get the wrong result if you are not careful.

Which should I use?

You can take advantage of both process maps and value stream maps, obviously due to the difference in the level of detail that's produced, so you want to make sure you create the right thing for the right reasons. Each type of map is used to identify different variables along the way, but there is value in combining the components of value streams with the detailed elements of process maps.

A detailed process map, if you think about it, does have all the elements of a value stream map – it can also be broken down into much greater detail.

> **Important Note**
> When your value stream map has identified waste, consider using a process map to include a much greater level of detail.

In the next section, we'll understand the difference between process mapping and value stream mapping. Let's finish this chapter by looking at an example of a value stream map and look at what we can do to improve our processes.

Explaining an example value stream map

So far in this chapter, we have looked at what value stream maps are, how they can help your business, and, at a high level, the components involved in your value stream map. Now, we'll start looking at how to build value stream maps, while also looking at the before and after states of DevOps processes.

The process of creating a value stream map that is meaningful can be a lengthy process, depending on how big the process is. As we discussed earlier, make sure you are getting something out of the process by monitoring your return on investment from your value stream mapping activities.

Creating a value stream map

When you start to create a value stream map, you should follow the following steps to ensure you are successful. It can be a tough task, creating a value stream map for the first time. Follow these steps and tips along the way and you will be able to produce value stream maps of true value.

Determining the problem to be solved

First, you need to determine what problem you are trying to solve. Don't try to map a value stream just because you want to make a diagram – create your value stream map from something where a problem exists.

To give you some insight into this, think of problem solving from your customer's perspective. Do they feel it takes you too long to deliver new features? Everyone will need to be on the same page, so make sure you publish your problem statement.

Finally, set some goals. It's not realistic to say you want to reduce it by a specific percentage; it's an admirable goal, but make sure it's realistic.

Ensuring the team is empowered

When working through value stream maps, you need a team that's both experienced and mature. This will help them navigate the task at hand and, most importantly, complete it in a timely manner. Leadership should also set aside the budget required to ensure that execution is in line with expectations.

Bounding the process

Once you have completed and published your problem statement, it is important to limit the scope of your value stream mapping exercise. You may not need to map the entire process end to end; you may only need to focus on a specific part of the process.

This process of breaking down complex processes into smaller parts and then breaking them down even more until the complexity is rendered in understandable, discreet components is known as process decomposition.

I would recommend this approach overall; you will get better results from experience by focusing on part of the problem rather than everything top to bottom. Tackle the full process in stages rather than end to end.

Once you have bounded your efforts to a part of the process, make sure you map it by conducting a review. Experience cannot be substituted by biased, incomplete, or even inaccurate documentation or narrative by others.

Define the steps of the process; complete this multiple times. Sometimes, things come out on the second or even third pass. Make sure you do this at least twice to ensure you get a complete picture.

Collecting process data and creating a timeline

While you are conducting your value stream mapping exercise, note down any applicable process data you wish to collect. This may include, but is certainly not limited to, the following information:

- Number of people involved
- Average working hours
- Cycle time
- Wait time
- Uptime

Also, make sure that you include your process times and lead times at the bottom. Remember earlier when I explained what the time ladder is used for? This is where it comes in.

Assessing the current value stream map

When you start to assess your current value stream map, look for specific things at this stage of the process. Ask the following questions:

- Do teams have multiple dependencies?
- Is your wait time or lead time too long?
- Might this be because your testing does not run in parallel?
- Is your environment stable?

All these questions can be used to evaluate your value stream map. It could even be that you have valuable steps in your process, but they don't transpire into anything meaningful to the customer. You should also be looking for any drag in the process or stagnation within the information flow. Make a note of whether this is either a push or a pull.

Designing your future state

At this stage, your value stream map may not be completed or a final version, but that's fine. The important thing here is to ensure that the value stream map for your future state aligns with your organization's vision for the future.

Make sure nothing is set in stone. In the spirit of DevOps as well, ensure you can incorporate continuous feedback into this process and make any adjustments that make sense.

Implementing your future state

You must validate that your future state is going to make the differences you envisage. Monitor your **objectives and key results** (**OKRs**), as well as your **key performance indicators** (**KPIs**), to learn from the trends you are seeing. We discussed metrics in *Chapter 3*, *Measuring the Success of DevOps*, which can be used to make KPIs.

> **Important Note**
> The goal of a successful value stream mapping exercise is ensuring that everyone is now pointing and working in the same direction: that of the customer.

Of course, all of this should have fixed the problem you set out in the problem statement you defined at the beginning. If you cannot say it has, then go back and look at what else can be done to make the situation better.

Current state value stream map

Now, let's look at a real example of what value stream maps look like in the DevOps world. Take a look at the following diagram, which is a template from *Lucidchart* (`https://www.lucidchart.com/pages/examples/value-stream-mapping-software`) that perfectly illustrates the value you can get:

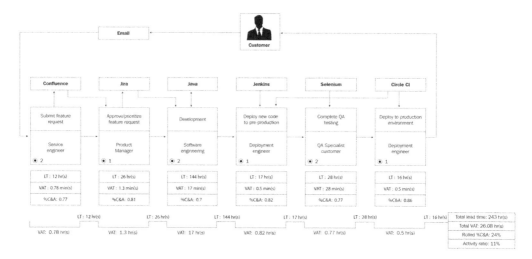

Figure 6.6 – Current value stream map of our DevOps processes

I want to take a little bit of time to explain what is happening in this diagram. First, let's discuss the process in a few words. You can see that our customer section is the main point of ingress.

It starts with the customer sending a feature request via email. This is picked up by one of two service engineers. At this point, they log that request into Confluence. The one product manager in the team then approves and prioritizes the feature request in Jira.

Then, our software engineering team of two people will work on that item in Java using the details from the request in *Jira*. That code is then deployed into pre-production by one deployment engineer using *Jenkins* and *Circle CI*. Then, using *Selenium*, QA is completed by QA specialists and the customer. Finally, one deployment engineer is responsible for pulling all the development effort together to release to production.

The total lead time for this process is 243 hours, while the total value-added time (the time spent on a task) is 26.08 hours. **%C&A** refers to the output that is complete and accurate, while **Rolled %C&A** (24%) refers to the time that does not need to be reworked. Finally, the **activity ratio**, at 11%, is the time spent working.

Overall, while the process is well-defined and mapped out well, you can see several areas of improvement. Let's look at these areas.

Future state value stream map

Future state does not always have to be about removing steps from your process. Remember that it is about making efficiency savings for your process. Look at the following future state value stream map:

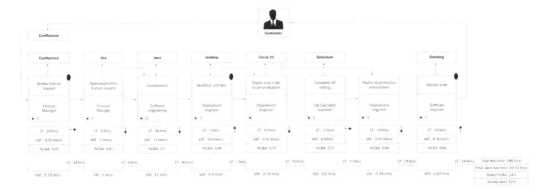

Figure 6.7 – Future state value stream map for our DevOps processes

Before I get into the details of what has changed with our future state, please see the dots above the top right of the process boxes, which indicate that a process is new. As I just mentioned, this is not about cutting process steps but adding them if this adds value.

Next, under each process, the time data shown includes arrows pointing right to indicate no change. You will add these if you introduce a new process. The arrows pointing down indicate a decrease in time from the previous value stream map or current process, while arrows pointing up indicate an increase in time.

So, let's have a look at what has changed. First, let's look at the new processes. Here, you can see that instead of having the customer send across an email with their new requirement, this is now fulfilled by the direct addition to **Confluence**. The product manager will now review and approve/prioritize the request, resulting in time being saved.

This also results in a reduction in lead time for the developers to complete their development effort, which is now down to 96 hours lead time and 11 minutes for completing the actual task.

In fact, you can see savings across several different tasks in the process and the introduction of new testing processes, as well as monitoring the code. All this means that the total lead time is now 188 hours, down from 243 hours.

The value added time is now 19.54 hours, down from 26.08 hours. We have reduced the amount of time people are working on value, which isn't a bad thing. This means they can deliver more with the time they have. Introducing testing and monitoring makes delivery more mature, but above all, increases the customer's interaction with us.

Summary

In this chapter, we looked at the process of value stream mapping, understood what it is, how it can help us, and how to build a value stream map. We also looked at the difference between value stream maps and process maps, discussed the different types of process waste you can identify in your processes, and finally looked at an example of how to create a value stream map.

In the next chapter, we will look at how to take what you have learned in this chapter and apply that to delivering process change in your organization. We'll do this by looking at eight steps for change, the effects of process change, and common challenges within process change.

Questions

Now, let's recap some of what we have learned throughout this chapter:

1. Which of these will you not find on a value stream map?

   a. Information flow

   b. Product flow

   c. Swim lane

   d. Time ladder

2. Which of these is not a type of waste?

   a. Transport

   b. Underproduction

   c. Motion

   d. Overproduction

7
Delivering Process Change in Your Organization

Now that you understand your processes and what needs to be changed, this chapter looks at how to manage process change across your organization. Remember that sometimes processes affect multiple teams and departments. This can be a challenge and needs to be carefully managed to ensure success.

By the end of this chapter, you will be able to understand the eight steps of effective process change, the different models of business change, and the common challenges of process change.

In this chapter, we're going to cover the following main topics:

- Eight steps for effective change
- Models for business change
- People effects of process change
- The common challenges of process change

Eight steps for effective change

In business, the need to change is fairly constant. Businesses that adapt to change effectively are ones that come out on top in the long run and beat their competition. When you have mapped out processes and completed value stream maps, your next task to undertake is to look at how to effectively deliver that change in your organization.

This starts with an eight-step plan for change, the steps of which can be described as follows:

1. Identifying what can be improved
2. Presenting a business case to stakeholders
3. Planning for change
4. Identifying resources and data for evaluation
5. Communicating
6. Evaluating resistance, dependencies, and risk
7. Celebrating success
8. Continuously improving

Some of these steps will be familiar to you already, since we have already discussed a few of them, but let's now have a look at them all in detail.

Identifying what will be improved

I have included this step here purely for completeness. For clarity, we covered this in the previous chapter, when talking about value stream maps, and discussed at length how to identify what needs to be improved and when something should be improved.

Knowing what you need to change will create a strong base for the successful implementation of a change to your process.

Presenting a business case to stakeholders

Presenting a business case to your stakeholders is the next step. However, this step might not be needed depending on how you have gone about gathering support for your change in process so far.

If you have already engaged your stakeholders and walked them through the problem statement and how it can be fixed, then you have essentially presented your business case.

Depending on the type of change and the impact on the wider business, don't be surprised if you find you have to present your idea to wider stakeholders to gather wider support.

Planning for change

Lots of people think that when you have your completed value stream map, you are good to go. Before you do anything, plan how you are going to implement your change. You stand a greater chance of success if you put the work into planning first.

It may be a small change you are making, but still set yourself clear goals about what success will look like when your change is implemented. It also goes without saying that if your change is large and touches numerous parts of your organization, then planning is key.

Identifying resources and data for evaluation

This step is part of your planning. Ensure you have the right resources to execute efficiently. Think about more than just people when it comes to resources. This could be additional software, training, tools, or documentation changes to name a few.

Data comes down to how you evaluate progress and success. Having appropriate data means you can provide data-informed updates on your progress and hopefully your success, rather than a feeling or gut instinct.

Communicating

Communication is the real key to success. It is the golden nugget that most change management frameworks have in common with each other. It runs through the entire practice of change management. It is that important.

Clear and open lines of communication are fundamental to your success in delivering process change. Communication methods allow you to have avenues to vent frustrations, celebrate what is working, and review what is not. Finally, communication is a key enabler of transparency that keeps everyone onside.

Evaluating resistance, dependencies, and risk

One of the biggest risks to the success of your change is resistance. It's normal and occurs in every organization. The majority of resistance occurs because of fear of the unknown. More generically, there is a level of risk associated with every change you make. Maybe it won't have the desired effects.

You can navigate resistance by arming your team and leadership with tools and knowledge to aid in a smooth transition.

Celebrating success

Recognize the small incremental changes along the way as well as the final success. Each step you make in the right direction is a positive one and each step should be celebrated. Your team will be working hard to make this successful, and celebrating their success and recognizing their efforts will keep people going, especially if the change is over a long period of time.

Continuously improving

Change management can be very difficult, as it is an ongoing process that needs tweaking when appropriate to help ensure success. **Continuous improvement** should be threaded through the entire process, just like communication. This can help you identify and resolve roadblocks along the way.

Now that we have explored these eight steps in more detail, let's look at some change management models you can use in your organization.

Models for business change

Many frameworks exist for executing change within your business, and like all frameworks, some will fit your business better than others. Some are for specific scenarios. You should never try to fit your business to the framework; rather, fit the framework to your business.

In this section, we are going to take a look at four business change models, how they can be used, and what they teach us. You may even take elements from multiple frameworks and put them into your own. The frameworks are as follows:

- **Kotter's change management model**
- **Rogers' tech adoption curve**
- The **Awareness, Desire, Knowledge, Ability, Reinforcement (ADKAR)** model
- **Envision, Activate, Support, Implement, Ensure, Recognize (EASIER)**

Let's look at each of these models in more detail.

Kotter's change management model

The first model is Kotter's change management model. This is the brainchild of *Dr. John Kotter* (`https://www.kotterinc.com/team/john-kotter`), who is an author and management consultant; he is a thought leader in business, leadership, and change and is the founder of Kotter International, which applies Kotter's leadership research to help organizations execute large-scale change. Like the model discussed earlier in this chapter, Kotter's model is also an eight-step model, which is split into three phases. These phases are as follows:

- Creating the climate for change
- Engaging and enabling the organization
- Implementing and sustaining for change

Steps one through three are the first phase, steps four through six are phase two, and finally, steps seven and eight are the final phase. The steps in the Kotter model are as follows:

1. Create urgency.
2. Form a powerful coalition.
3. Create a vision for change.
4. Communicate the vision.
5. Empower action.
6. Create quick wins.
7. Build on the change.
8. Make it stick.

Kotter introduced this eight-step model in 1995. Kotter lays out that even if one of the preceding steps were to fail, the whole change initiative will fail. The following diagram is a visual representation of the model:

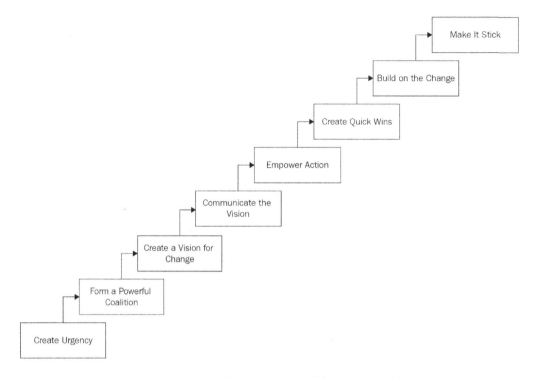

Figure 7.1 – Visual representation of the Kotter model

One of the major benefits of Kotter's model is that the steps are actionable and in the form of a checklist. It's a step-by-step model that is clear to follow, with detailed descriptions of the steps along the way.

It has a limitation, though, in that it lacks any steps for measurement and is time consuming to implement. Scholars have also pointed out over time that it is a fluid process that does not follow any linear path.

Rogers' technology adoption curve

A slightly different take on the change management model is the technology adoption curve. The model is used to define an adoption timeframe and has some uses in popular culture.

Simon Sinek talks about the technology adoption curve in his now-famous TED talk *Start with Why* (`https://www.ted.com/talks/simon_sinek_how_great_leaders_inspire_action`). Sinek refers to this as the *Law of Diffusion of Innovation*.

Developed by George Beal, Everett Rogers, and Joe Bohlen in 1957, the original application was for agriculture, but it was later applied to technology. The technology adoption curve aims to highlight the levels of acceptance of new ideas in society through five distinct stages:

1. Innovators
2. Early adopters
3. Early majority
4. Late majority
5. Laggards

The curve explains how your idea would be successful regarding adoption. Your idea is not going to be successful if you try to convince the late majority to accept your idea. The *Diffusion of Innovations* talks about the gap between early adopters and the early majority; bridging that gap is key to achieving success.

> **Tip**
> When adopting DevOps, target the innovators and early adopters in your organization to get support and bring them on the journey. Then, work with the early majority to tip the balance of support.

Apply this same principle of change with DevOps methodologies. When you are trying to drive the adoption of your change strategy for DevOps, make sure you target the innovators and early adopters, then the early majority, within your organization.

I am a big fan of this model and have used it successfully in several different scenarios. That said, if you are looking for a traditional framework, then this is not the answer for you.

The ADKAR model

The ADKAR model (`https://www.prosci.com/adkar/adkar-model`) is one that is goal-oriented. The model was created by Jeff Hiatt, who is the founder of *Prosci*. The company focuses on customer success and is represented around the world.

ADKAR is an acronym that represents five tangible outcomes that need to be achieved for lasting change within the organization. Those five outcomes are as follows:

- Awareness

- Desire

- Knowledge

- Ability

- Reinforcement

The model closely follows the steps of Kotter's model as well in its own way. Similarly, the ADKAR model is also aligned in three phases as well, which are **Current**, **Transition**, and **Future**.

The model rewards individual change within the organizational change framework. However, the downside of the model is that in larger organizations, it is cumbersome.

The EASIER model

The EASIER model follows six broad steps. It was introduced by David Hussey. You can see similarities in the steps Hussey describes in his model with other frameworks.

The six steps that make the EASIER model are as follows:

1. Envision

2. Activate

3. Support

4. Implement

5. Ensure

6. Recognize

A limitation of this framework is the heavy reliance on leadership effectiveness and response. A solid benefit though is the checklist-style approach to change management, which makes it popular with many people, much like the Kotter model.

Now, we have looked at the models for business change and how we can use them for our organizations. Let's now look at the effects of process change.

People effects of process change

People are the beating heart of your organization. Have people on board. Your organizational change will likely have a greater chance of success over one where people are disengaged.

When you go through any organizational change, especially ones that may change the roles and responsibilities of the people involved, it is important to consider the effects of this on the people within your organization, not just those directly affected, but the ones who are indirectly affected as well.

Direct impact

When we talk about direct impact, we mean employees who are directly affected by the changes you are proposing. This includes people whose roles and/or responsibilities will change as a result of your proposal.

Of course, by far the biggest impact you will have comes directly in the form of resistance. We discussed in *Chapter 5*, *Avoiding Cultural Anti-Patterns in DevOps*, that the reasons for resistance are as follows:

- Fear of losing your job
- Poor communication
- Lack of trust
- Fear of the unknown
- Poor timing

Those are great reasons, certainly common in my experience, but what about other effects of direct impact? Consider the following effects:

- Pushing people out of their comfort zone
- Disruption to social arrangements
- Lowering of status

Let's now look at these three reasons in more detail.

Pushing people out of their comfort zone

Throughout your career, you start to get comfortable with what you do. Some people relish the idea of going out of their comfort zone, but others don't like this at all. Don't assume everyone in your organization cannot wait to get outside of their comfort zone; the reality is that most people don't want that.

So, one of the consequences of direct impact changes is that people feel as though they are being pushed outside of their comfort zone. For someone who doesn't like this arrangement, this will be unsettling. You need to address this before it results in people leaving the organization.

We've discussed quite a bit the importance of communication and transparency. Both are key here – you may not be able to resolve every conflict in this area, but good communication and transparency will make it much easier.

Disruption to social arrangements

History as well as most management articles tell us that work-life balance is incredibly important to the mental health of your employees. Part of this balance is the social arrangements employees make with circles inside and outside of the office.

Anything that appears to disrupt this will also make people nervous and question the validity of the change. Yes, this is a form of resistance, like the other two reasons we are exploring, but you would be shocked to find the number of times this is overlooked.

If you are working in a large organization over multiple geographies, don't forget the cultural aspect. Your changes may have a negative impact on important dates in one culture's calendar but be harmless for your own.

Lowering of status

Most people will tell you that job title and status within the business is not important. However, as pointed out in this article on *Glassdoor* (`https://www.glassdoor.com/blog/the-importance-of-title-in-the-job-search-process`), job titles over time help show career progression, reflect salary, and potentially determine future roles. So, anything that can suppress that progression by reflecting a lowering of status is something potential employers will question.

For this reason, be careful when you are working with changes that impact roles and responsibilities. You can end up making it seem like someone has got a demotion, judging by a change to their title; hopefully this isn't your intention.

Now that we understand the direct impact, let's have a look at the indirect impact and effects on people.

Indirect impact

In contrast to direct impact, think of indirect impact as a situation where a team that is directly impacted by the change does some critical work for another team; that other team is now indirectly impacted by the changes you are making.

> **Important note**
> Organizations often consider direct impact and deal with it well, but not indirect impact. This indirect impact can end up making your change fail, so consider the consequences carefully.

Dealing with indirect impact can be tricky, as you might not even know about it until it's become a problem and you have to fix it. Identifying such impacts early can be crucial to overall success.

Some examples of indirect impact could be as follows:

- Health of employees
- Shadow IT
- Process dependencies

Let's look at these three reasons in more detail to understand them better.

Health of employees

We briefly discussed mental wellbeing in terms of work-life balance, but this goes further than that. It's about the overall health of your employees. Sudden changes in working conditions, environment, and other factors can have an adverse effect on your health.

Carefully consider the health impact of the changes you are making. It may be that there are none, but it's still important to consider it. Employees will also appreciate the fact it has been discussed and considered as well.

Shadow IT

We all know and have experienced **shadow IT**. This is where separate teams are doing their own services and running their own tooling outside of the control of central IT teams. Be incredibly careful with this.

It's not unusual for shadow IT to be responsible for a business-critical service, and for a change to cause issues with the stability of that service because the team's responsibilities are disrupted.

Managing shadow IT without causing disruption to innovation in your organization is a tricky balance. For some ideas on how to manage this, look at this article from *TechRepublic* (`https://www.techrepublic.com/article/5-tips-for-managing-shadow-it-without-destroying-innovation`) on how to manage shadow IT.

Shadow IT has a huge impact on personnel in your organization. Shadow IT is usually work that is untracked and unaccounted for, so it is often done alongside people's day-to-day roles.

Process dependencies

Even if you go down the route of creating value stream maps or running through process maps within your organization, you may miss dependencies between processes. You miss these dependencies if they are manual hand-offs.

For that reason, it's important to speak to the right people when creating your value stream or process maps. Make multiple passes to ensure you capture all the manual hand-offs so that you reduce the risk of missing process dependencies.

The risk here is that by missing one of these dependencies, when you change the master process you will break something else downstream. This then has an adverse effect on people downstream: it can increase their workload or it can put undue pressure on them to resolve an issue that may not be fixable now that you have changed something.

Now let's have a look at some of the common challenges of process change within organizations.

The common challenges of process change

Implementing a change management framework, such as one of the ones we discussed earlier in *Models for business change*, comes with its own set of challenges, and sometimes these challenges can be quite complex.

Here are several common challenges that are prohibitive to process change:

- Organizational resistance
- Lack of established goals
- Poor strategic alignment

- Starting with tools
- Underestimating the need for change frameworks
- The domino effect

Let's look at these in more detail to understand their impact. We won't discuss organizational resistance as we've already discussed this previously.

Lack of established goals

Goals are critical. You must have defined goals, so you know how to measure your success and know the direction in which you are heading. When you do not establish goals, it is hard to know which direction you are heading in, and you can lose your way quickly.

When you establish clear and well-defined goals, everyone knows where they need to head; everyone knows what success looks like.

Poor strategic alignment

Strategic alignment, or lack of it, kills change management. You must gain clear strategic alignment with all stakeholders. Not having clear strategic alignment results in a failed transformation project.

One method to achieve strong strategic alignment could be following these steps:

1. Start at the top – goal setting must start with the executive team.
2. Create a cascade of goals.
3. Drive consistency and accountability.
4. Encourage continuous communication.

What does this mean? Strategic alignment is making sure that the process changes align with the business goals. When you have a mismatch between the two is where you have issues later down the line. When you are aligned, expect a smoother change process.

Starting with tools

I'm a passionate believer that when you start with any tool related to DevOps, you are destined for failure. You must consider culture, people, and processes first.

Implementing tools before you understand the problem is a disaster waiting to happen. When it comes to tools and processes, and especially automation, you are enabling poor processes to run faster. Work on them first before implementing tools.

Good alignment and strategy on enterprise architecture is also important. With so many tools available, it's easy to get lost and deploy whichever tools appear to fix the problem. Before long, you have a plethora of tools in your environment. Enterprise architecture looks to implement standards and processes and align standard sets of requirements for new software.

These requirements are key when it comes to implementing new tools in your organization.

Underestimating the need for change frameworks

In general, when the impact of change initiatives on people is ignored by organizations, roadblocks arise, and the desired results are not achieved. For process management, many organizations have limited staff involvement. Employees who don't understand, care for, or even agree with the process are limited in commitment. Employee engagement builds employee support and overcomes corporate resistance.

The domino effect

Organizations that report that their process management efforts do not have pre-established goals will likely face further challenges, such as the lack of strategic alignment, insufficient communication, and the lack of IT tools. This second set of challenges leads to several challenges in managing change, including resistance to the organization and the need for change management.

Summary

In this chapter, we looked at how to effectively implement change within your organization. As part of this, we looked at eight simple steps to help achieve this and four change models used in organizations to help change be effective. We also looked at the direct and indirect effects that process change has on people within an organization. Finally, we looked at the common challenges you may face when implementing change within organizations.

Next, we will look at the continuous improvement of processes – how do you improve your processes when you have gone through the improvement process already? We will look at some techniques for continuous improvement, how to iterate changes to processes, and how to keep pace with change.

Questions

Let's now recap some of what we have learned throughout this chapter:

1. Which model helps define a timeline rather than implement a framework?

    a. Rogers' technology adoption curve

    b. The ADKAR model

    c. Kotter's change management model

    d. The EASIER model

2. What is generally the most important step for effective change?

    a. Identifying what needs to be improved

    b. Improvement

    c. Communication

    d. Celebrating success

8

Continuous Improvement of Processes

Continuous feedback and improvement is a key element of DevOps. The ability to keep learning and providing feedback on all aspects of DevOps to further improve what you are doing and provide more value to the business is a fundamental pillar of DevOps. This chapter looks at the techniques for continuous feedback, how to iterate process changes, and ensuring everyone stays up to date with changes.

In this chapter, we're going to cover the following main topics:

- What is continuous improvement and feedback?
- Techniques for continuous improvement and feedback
- Iterating changes to processes
- Keeping pace with change

What is continuous improvement and feedback?

Continuous improvement is the process of ongoing effort required to improve services, products, or processes. This process can be done in an iterative manner over a period or all at once. How this is done is dependent on the degree of change we are looking to make.

Continuous feedback has many different uses, including the ability to provide feedback to employees on their performance. You can also use continuous feedback in product development to gain valuable insights into the performance of your product. The systematic way that strengths and weaknesses of employee performance are discussed translates well to the product world and DevOps as well.

Let's now look at continuous improvement in more detail.

Building a continuous improvement culture

The concept of DevOps is primarily built around continuous everything. Lots of terminology in DevOps also includes it in the name, such as continuous integration, and continuous deployment to name a couple. Continuous everything is a great level to achieve, and things like continuous integration, testing, and deployment work towards removing bottlenecks in software delivery processes and tools.

Continuous improvement, however, looks at the removal of bottlenecks in DevOps systems and processes. Creating a culture of continuous improvement is not specific to technology or DevOps though.

Building a successful continuous improvement culture is all about making sure you instill the principles at each level of leadership. As time progresses, you should make noise about your successes; you have to fight the inertia and reluctance to change processes and routines, even the bad ones.

Let's now look at continuous feedback in more detail. Many industries already have well-developed practices and methodologies around continuous improvement. We can take a lot of learnings from the manufacturing industry, where lean was born. In lean, continuous improvement is called **Kaizen**. Let's discuss this in more detail.

Understanding and implementing Kaizen principles

Kaizen was born over 30 years ago thanks to Masaaki Imai, the founder of the *Kaizen Institute* (`https://www.kaizen.com`). Today, Kaizen is recognized as a key pillar when it comes to competitive advantage.

Kaizen is built on five principles:

- **Know your customer** – Determine their interests so that you can improve their experience.

- **Let it flow** – Everyone in your organization should strive to add value while reducing waste.

- **Go to gemba** – Value is created where things happen.

- **Empower people** – Performance and improvements should be tangible and visible.

- **Be transparent** – Set the same goals for your teams and provide a system and tools to reach them.

One of the most famous implementations of Kaizen is the **Toyota Production System** or **TPS** for short (`https://en.wikipedia.org/wiki/Toyota_Production_System`). The expectation is that when an anomaly is detected, all production personnel stop what they are doing and suggest an improvement to resolve the issue. This may then initiate Kaizen.

The cycle of Kaizen, known as a blitz, burst, or event is based on **PDCA**, or the Deming cycle, and defines four steps:

1. **Plan**
2. **Do**
3. **Check**
4. **Act**

The fundamental concept of this is to identify any waste in the system and quickly remove it. In *Chapter 7, Delivering Process Change in Your Organization*, on driving process change with value stream maps, one of the symbols we discussed was the initiation of a Kaizen burst. If you think back to that chapter, then think about what we have discussed here, this is where you can see the link between the two activities.

The value stream map is used to map out and identify the activities and the waste, then the Kaizen burst is used to eliminate that waste. It is the burst that is the activity performed to resolve the waste and implement a new process.

Another common continuous improvement model is *Six Sigma* (`https://en.wikipedia.org/wiki/Six_Sigma`). Kaizen and Six Sigma are the two models you will often find in DevOps, used to continuously improve processes.

The main difference is that Kaizen seeks to improve the business as a whole by establishing a standard way of working, increasing efficiency, and eliminating business waste.

Six Sigma is more concerned with output quality (the final product). This is made possible by identifying and eliminating the sources of defects.

Lean is all about eliminating waste in order to increase process speed and quality by reducing process waste.

Let's now look at how to build a culture of continuous feedback at your organization.

Building a continuous feedback culture

Carrying on from our theme of continuous everything when it comes to DevOps, if continuous improvement is the methodology used to improve your processes and systems, then continuous feedback is the mechanism that highlights that opportunity for change.

Like continuous improvement, continuous feedback is not a DevOps exclusive idea or model but also takes inspiration from the employee management world. Continuous feedback can be considered informal, however, tools and processes do exist to define how the feedback is collected, processed, and even acted upon:

*   Clear communication of vision and goals
*   Understanding the purpose of continuous feedback
*   Providing channels and tools to share feedback
*   Ensuring accountability for the feedback given and received
*   Educating teams about the importance of continuous feedback

Let's now look at these five key elements of continuous feedback culture in more detail.

Clear communication of vision and goals

Without clear communication of your organization's vision and goals, it's hard for your teams to contribute feedback on how to improve. When your teams clearly understand vision and goals, it makes it easy for them to provide quality feedback on the things that need to change.

Feedback, when you understand the context of both the vision and goals, allows your teams to directly think about what parts of processes, systems, and tools need to change to enable your organization to have a greater chance of achieving its goals.

Understanding the purpose of continuous feedback

Providing good feedback is not simply about just saying "good job" or "you didn't execute well enough." Good feedback provides tangible examples with a detailed explanation. It should be as descriptive as possible and as real-time as possible.

Feedback allows for the management of performance. This is irrespective of either individuals or assets such as products or services. Feedback helps identify areas of both improvement and strength, which with feedback can be respectively made better or even stronger.

> **Tip**
> Continuous feedback should not just come from leaders. It should come from everyone and be treated the same no matter where it comes from.

From your team's perspective, this also provides the ability for them to voice their opinions and concerns in a constructive manner, especially when you are starting out on your DevOps transformation. This is a useful way to engage everyone.

Providing channels and tools to share feedback

Providing several ways, known as channels, to share feedback is crucial. Everyone likes to engage in a different way. You will find some people use one channel and others use another.

Individual feedback sessions, as well as group feedback sessions, give a great balance and you will find that you will get great feedback from both sessions. One of the benefits of group feedback sessions is that you will find that feedback from one person may spur on similar feedback or validation of that feedback. This can be a powerful exercise.

Don't discount the power of anonymous feedback. While it would be great to attribute every piece of great feedback to an individual, even in culturally mature environments, the truth is that people sometimes want to provide feedback anonymously. There is nothing wrong with this approach and anonymous feedback should be welcomed and actioned the same way.

Ensuring accountability for the feedback given and received

Regardless of whether your feedback is anonymous or not, it's key that someone is accountable for that feedback, both if you are providing feedback and if you are receiving feedback. You need to own that feedback. Everyone needs to be committed to the culture of continuous feedback.

Consistency is required for feedback to change a culture. It helps drive accountability and transparency horizontally and vertically. Make sure the feedback is public. The actions you take and, if possible, the decisions you made to decide on the appropriate action to take, should be public.

Educating teams about the importance of continuous feedback

One thing you cannot do or expect is to implement a system of continuous feedback and have teams and employees get it overnight. Training and communication are important here as both in tandem allow you to highlight the reasons why you are doing the scheme, what the benefits will be, and how it will work.

Highlight to employees that both positive and negative feedback is equal. Both positive and negative feedback helps you improve, regardless of whether that is employee performance, product performance, or service performance.

Now we understand what continuous feedback and improvement are. Let's now look at the techniques we can use to implement them within our organization.

Techniques for continuous improvement and feedback

When we looked at *What is continuous improvement and feedback?* at the start of the chapter, we briefly discussed the use of Kaizen and there was a quick mention of Six Sigma, which are both methodologies you can use to take steps towards continuous improvement. What about before you get to that stage though?

Let's now look at techniques you can use for continuous improvement.

Continuous improvement processes

As we discussed in the previous section, the PDSA cycle stands for Plan, Do, Study, and Act. Behind this is a six-step model that is a systematic approach to planning, sequencing, and improving efforts using data and is an elaboration of the PDSA model.

The six steps used are as follows:

1.   Identify opportunities

2.   Analyze the root cause

3.   Take action

4.   Study the results

5. Standardize the solution

6. Plan for the future

These distinct steps are sequential and an essential part of a continuous improvement process. Your continuous improvement plans should always link back to your organization's vision, goals, and priorities.

Let's have a look at these six steps in more detail.

Identify opportunities

You can identify opportunities for process improvement in a few different ways. An opportunity is likely to come from continuous feedback where a problem is highlighted and the result of that is the opportunity to improve.

It could also come from personal feedback from the team working with the process, or in less mature environments, where the continuous feedback loop is not yet fully established but an operational issue or complaint has triggered that review.

Analyze the root cause

Before you can start to remediate the problem, you need to understand what the problem is. Make sure you identify the root cause of the problem. Remember, in some cases, issues occur because of a chain of events, so don't stop at the first problem you find. Keep looking backward to find the earliest issue that could have set off a chain reaction of events.

The analysis does not stop there though. When you know what the root cause is, validate those findings and see what you can do to prove that is indeed the root cause. Depending on the process, and of course the inputs, you may even be able to reproduce the results.

Take action

When you are ready to act, this is a two-step process. First, you need to be able to plan the actions that correct the root cause. Bear in mind, there could be numerous actions needed to resolve the problem.

The second step is implementing those planned actions. Implementing that plan comes with several actions. Communicating your plan is crucial here. Having the right people in place is also important to help make the changes successful.

Study the results

Confirming the actions you have taken and implemented is also important. You need to monitor associated metrics with the process you have changed and any associated outputs and tooling to make sure that your changes have worked and have not had an adverse effect.

Be prepared through your planning to have a route to back out of the changes should they be unsuccessful and to make small incremental changes if needed to make your changes successful.

Standardize the solution

Through regular monitoring, you can see whether the results you are seeing are consistent and established. At this point, you must ensure that the improved level of performance is consistently maintained.

Sometimes you will need to make further changes to make this standardized approach stick across the whole organization. You should make sure you plan for those things as well.

Plan for the future

When you have completed your implementation, take a step back. A simple retrospective will help here. Work with the team to identify what went well. This is a form of continuous feedback and what you learn here can be applied next time you make a process change.

Any residual problems that come out of the change need to be accounted and planned for here as well.

Now we have looked at the six steps involved in continuous improvement, let's have a look at other continuous improvement techniques you can use in your organization.

Additional continuous improvement techniques

We have just walked through one example of a continuous improvement process that you can use in your organization to help get started. Of course, plenty of other frameworks and techniques exist though. Let's have a look at some of them.

Daily huddles

One of the most common agile practices that almost all organizations will practice is the daily huddle, sometimes known as the daily standup. Your daily huddle can be a source of inspiration for identifying opportunities to improve.

Having the whole team on that short call to discuss impediments will give people the opportunity to have their say about things that can be done to remove that impediment, which might even be a Kaizen burst to resolve a bottleneck.

Catchball

This is a lean technique that involves the movement of ideas from one person or a team to another one for feedback. Strictly speaking, this could also be a continuous feedback technique.

This method means people at different levels of the organization get to provide feedback and contribute to the development of that idea. It could be anything as well – in DevOps, this is commonly a product or service.

Gemba walks

You may not have heard of gemba walks, but you'll most likely have seen them done before. The practice involves leaders walking around, asking questions, and identifying opportunities for improvement with the people on the ground executing the work.

Improvements that are found are not implemented at this stage. This is done after analysis is done.

Now we have looked at some other continuous improvement techniques you can use in your organization, let's move on to looking at the continuous feedback process in more detail.

The continuous feedback process

In very simple terms, continuous feedback or a continuous feedback loop can be simplified as four simple steps. These four steps are as follows:

1. Assess
2. Modify
3. Plan
4. Implement

It won't come as a shock to you that the four steps outlined above have very close relationships with the continuous improvement process we discussed earlier. You can connect both processes together though.

The process outlined above for continuous feedback ensures you have the appropriate process in place to capture feedback, assess what that feedback means, plan how it is going to be actioned, and then implement that plan. This is where continuous improvement comes in.

Let's now look at other continuous feedback techniques you can use within your organization.

Additional continuous feedback techniques

Most continuous feedback techniques come from the employee performance management world and human resources. You can use a number of those techniques for product and service feedback though.

Let's look at some of them.

The EDGE framework

The founder of Zoomly *Dawn Sillett* (`https://www.zoomly.co.uk/people`) outlines the **EDGE** feedback framework. It is an acronym for **Explain, Describe, Give**, and **End Positively**, this provides a clear structure that aims to improve clarity and provides actionable results from that feedback.

Each component of the framework is aimed at improving performance in a sustained manner.

360-degree feedback

You will have come across 360-degree feedback in your time. This is the task of collecting feedback from multiple sources to build up a bigger picture of performance. In human terms, this is from leaders, managers, colleagues, and peers.

In the DevOps world, this can be from different product managers, engineers, security teams, customers, and other sources. Think about whether you want your 360-degree feedback to be anonymous or not. This is an important factor when it comes to quality.

Cross-team feedback is great, but remember, not all teams have the same culture. Without a mechanism to provide anonymous feedback, some people may not be as honest as they could be.

Feedback ratios

Different research suggests that the ratio of positive to negative feedback should be between 3:1 and 5:1. This is of course when working with humans, but feedback on processes, products, or services is similar.

Regardless of which ratio you work with, ensure that you heavily load feedback with positives over negatives. Emphasis on positive feedback helps create a culture of improvement and performance.

Now we have looked at the continuous feedback techniques available to us in our business, let's now look at how to iterate changes to your processes.

Iterating changes to processes

Just like with application code, it is important to take an iterative approach to changing processes. When it comes to application code, we take this approach so that if something does go wrong, we can easily know what changes were made, who made them, and why. It provides full traceability of what is happening.

We need that same level of traceability and transparency when it comes to iterating changes to processes. That way, if at any point we need to see what happened and why, it's easy to identify that information. Secondly, we can see the impact of a change before moving onto the next one.

This really applies to all types of changes, from technology processes to business processes. The biggest impact does not come with individual changes to those processes, but large programs of change that involve numerous changes to the same set of processes or the same process.

When we work in iterations, or in sprints as we commonly call them in agile methodologies, the results are clear, impactful, and wide-ranging across several disciplines. In fact, iterative design is commonly adopted as a design methodology in the prototyping, testing, analyzing, and refinement of a product. Why not apply this in process design as well?

Iterative design processes

When designing new processes, just like in product design, remember that changes are easier to make and less expensive to implement in the earliest stages of the development cycle.

In iterative design, the first step is to create a prototype. You can do the same with a process as well. Using all the requirements you have and the tools at your disposal, work on a prototype process and work through scenarios, documenting the outcomes, which is valuable feedback on how your process works.

Focus groups are used in iterative design processes as well. Just like gaining 360-degree feedback, or some of the elements of Kaizen, they work to gain feedback from specific groups of people on specific problems.

Iterative design is usually a continual process. The techniques we have discussed so far in this chapter have taught us the elements of this continual process.

Using iterative design

Iterative design is a way to face the realities of unpredictable user needs and behaviors, which can lead to major changes in the design. User testing often shows, when confronted with a user test, that even carefully assessed ideas are insufficient. It is therefore important that the flexibility of the iterative design approach is, as far as possible, extended to the system. Designers must also recognize that user testing results can lead to fundamental changes that require designers to be prepared to give up their old ideas in favor of more user-friendly new ideas.

Benefits of iterative design

When correctly applied, iterative design is a way of making sure that the best possible solution is in place. Significant cost savings are also possible when the iterative design approach is applied early in the development cycle.

Some other key benefits include the following:

- Misinterpretations become evident earlier in the process
- It encourages user feedback
- The development focuses on issues most critical to the project
- Inconsistencies between the design and requirements are detected early

We have looked at some techniques for continuous improvement and feedback in this section. Next, we will look at how to keep pace with change in your organization.

Keeping pace with change

On top of an individual's day-to-day role, it can be difficult keeping up with the technology changes in their field, as well as all the work they are doing in the current sprint, thinking about future work coming up as well. It's hard, so adding on top of that the process changes you are making makes it very difficult.

You need to be able to manage the pace of change within your organization when it comes to process changes. Of course, process changes are very important – they are how you improve as an organization, but they can be the thing people forget the quickest.

Process changes usually fail because the change fails to stick in the organization. With lots of competing priorities in most organizations and lots of information to keep on top of, many people sadly forget process information first.

The following things can be used to try and make this easier for your employees and make your process changes stick:

- Effective communication
- Knowledge transfer
- Access to subject matter experts

Let's now have a look at these three areas in more detail.

Effective communication

Having an effective method of communication is part of making your process changes stick in your organization.

Working groups

As a working group that is implementing a change to a process, you can set up sessions throughout the process to ensure that the changes you are making are bite-sized and that you communicate them frequently.

People are more likely to consume smaller chunks of information, especially when they have a high workload. Consider setting up working groups in person and virtually to maximize attendance.

Collaboration tools

Collaboration tools such as Microsoft Teams or Slack are effective at grouping together communication on such important topics. You can use the channels or groups concept to create a process group. Have everyone check this periodically and make wider announcements.

One of the benefits of this method is the communications and information you share are available for people to look back on. The drawback to attending meetings is people don't always make notes. Collaboration tools can fix this by making sure you have historical information available to view.

Group-wide emails

From experience, group-wide, generic emails to many people don't work. The communication isn't personal enough to engage people and have them look at the content properly.

If you do take this approach, consider something to make it more targeted rather than a blanket communication, to keep people engaged.

Knowledge transfer

The transfer of knowledge is important. We just discussed the use of collaboration tools. Use them to help transfer knowledge and keep documentation stored centrally so that there is one master version of truth for all process documents and flowcharts.

Everyone takes in information differently and it's important that you cater for these scenarios, but try to make sure that above all, this knowledge is stored centrally. Wikis are great tools to help with this and they're open to everyone to edit where applicable.

Access to subject matter experts

Having appropriate documentation and methods of communication and knowledge transfer is of course important, as we have just discussed. One of the simplest things you can do though is to make sure your subject matter experts have time to work with people who need help.

A common way of doing this I have implemented before that works well is to have your subject matter experts sit with the teams affected, so if they have a question, they can just ask – no need to raise a formal ticket and wait for a response over email.

Added benefits to this are that you increase the collaboration between people within your organization and this has longer-term benefits the more people work together. It helps establish an open culture and creates trust in turn.

Summary

In this chapter, we looked at the topics of continuous improvement and continuous feedback. We looked at Kaizen principles and how to build an effective continuous improvement and feedback culture in your organization. We also discussed how to iterate changes to your processes with iterative design processes, as well as how to keep pace with the rate of change in your organization.

The skills learned in this chapter will help you and your team continuously improve along your DevOps journey, not just during the initial transformation but, as we discussed, during the ongoing evolution of DevOps within your organization.

In the next chapter, we'll look at the technical stack for DevOps. We'll look at the groups of DevOps tools available, understand how tooling helps in DevOps, and the pros and cons of DevOps tools.

Questions

Let's now recap some of what we have learned throughout this chapter:

1. How do continuous improvement and feedback differ?

    a. Continuous feedback is about gathering rather than acting

    b. Continuous improvement is about acting on the feedback

    c. The models are the same

    d. The models are completely different

2. What design process aligns well with process change?

    a. Unit testing

    b. Iterative design

    c. Continuous deployment

    d. Continuous integration

Section 4: Implementing and Deploying DevOps Tools

Tooling adds to the value you have attained so far, but it is important to make sure that you do this in a strategic way and understand the steps involved.

This part of the book comprises the following chapters:

- *Chapter 9, Understanding the Technical Stack for DevOps*
- *Chapter 10, Developing a Strategy for Implementing Tooling*
- *Chapter 11, Keeping Up with Key DevOps Trends*
- *Chapter 12, Implementing DevOps in a Real-World Organization*

9
Understanding the Technical Stack for DevOps

Adding tooling to your DevOps investments is key to making sure your adoption goes from good to great. There are many DevOps tools on the market today. Understanding what toolsets to implement for today and for tomorrow can be challenging. In this chapter, we look at the pros and cons of the main tooling involved in DevOps.

By the end of this chapter, you can expect to gain an understanding of the different families of DevOps tools as well as understanding how tooling helps in DevOps. You will also understand the benefits and obstacles of DevOps tooling.

In this chapter, we're going to cover the following main topics:

- What are the families of DevOps tools?
- How does tooling help the adoption of DevOps?
- Understanding the benefits of DevOps tooling
- Understanding the obstacles of DevOps tooling

What are the families of DevOps tools?

The DevOps ecosystem, as we call it, has a number of different categories that tools fall into. Some of these tools are designed, developed, and marketed for incredibly specific reasons. There are industry-specific tools that solve unique problems as well.

Of course, you also come across tools that, while specific to a category, also apply across many industries, and some tools are suites of tools that provide services right across the ecosystem.

We can use a traditional diagram that depicts the DevOps loop to talk about the different categories. I like to use the following categories, which closely align to those given in traditional diagrams but have slight differences:

- Collaborating
- Building
- Testing
- Deploying
- Running

You can see a visual depiction of this in the following diagram:

Figure 9.1 – Visual representation of the toolchain phases

Let's have a look at these in more detail to understand what types of tools are part of each section of the ecosystem.

Collaborating

I have added collaboration to this list, which is not actually found on most traditional lists, because of the importance that collaboration has in DevOps. So far, we have looked at collaboration from a cultural perspective as well as when it comes to people and processes, but tooling is important to collaboration as well.

You can have great processes, people, and culture within your organization around collaboration, but in the end, without the right tools in place, you still won't get very far, and scaling will also be a real issue.

When you think of collaboration, it's easy to think of the big players such as Zoom, Microsoft Teams, Skype, and others, but the toolset is much broader than that. Collaboration is also about knowledge sharing.

Tools such as Read the Docs, GitHub Pages, and Apiary are all documentation tools; they are also classed as collaboration tools.

Knowledge sharing is important in any organization, but in teams where there is a high level of collaboration and a concerted move toward DevOps practices, knowledge is incredibly important. Every bit of knowledge about your product should be noted down and stored centrally so it can be found should anyone need it.

> **Tip**
> Think of knowledge management as a way to avoid knowledge silos. Without these silos in place, you are able to scale much better and ensure that everyone has an equal opportunity to learn new skills and learn more about the product.

Knowledge also includes documentation. In my opinion, you cannot consider something to be completed if no documentation exists for it. This documentation may be public-facing or it may be just for internal teams. Either way, it is important.

Building

Build tools are what enable you to take what you have developed and turn it into something that you can later deploy somewhere else. This starts with source control tooling. By far the most common such tool today is **Git**. It comes in a number of flavors, and one of the most popular is GitHub, although the Git technology is to be found within a number of different source control products.

Tooling also enables continuous integration. This practice entails taking your artifacts from your source control repository and running them through an automated workflow called a pipeline. During the pipeline, a number of tasks are completed, and the result of that pipeline is a tangible artifact that you can then later deploy.

Build tools are also not exclusively related to software. You can also build infrastructure with some tools as well. This is known as infrastructure as code. If you are using containers, you will also find tools to help you build them.

If your application involves the use of a database, you will also find database tooling available to you to manage your database schema and structure.

Testing

Testing is one of the broadest terms when it comes to DevOps tooling. Here you will find tools to perform testing for a wide range of requirements. The process of testing could be anything from the unit testing of code by developers all the way through to user acceptance testing and tools that automate browser testing for web applications.

In addition to this, testing can include security scanning your application against baselines from the OWASP Top 10, static and dynamic code analysis for vulnerabilities, and load testing to ensure your application performs well under load.

Deploying

The act of deployment is where you can take your built and tested application artifact and deploy it to where it needs to go. This could be to a cloud platform such as Microsoft Azure, Amazon Web Services, or Google Cloud. It could also be a mobile app store or even an on-premises data center.

If you are deploying to a cloud platform or app store, then you will likely be using native tooling to deploy to those environments. Those tools will probably only perform the deployment to those specific environments for you and nothing else.

You could also be deploying to a package management repository if you are writing sharable application libraries for other developers to use. You can also get tools that support this scenario.

If you are working with containers, then you are also likely to be working with artifact management tools; these come under the deployment banner as well. Tools that enable you to point your containers to container registries, either public or private, are accessed at this point.

Finally, even if you are provisioning and deploying virtual machines or other types of traditional infrastructure, you may use tools responsible for baseline configuration management or provisioning your infrastructure. These tools can save huge amounts of time when it comes to managing enterprise-scale infrastructure.

Running

Once you have deployed your application, you have entered what is known as the run phase. At this point, the operations team uses tooling to manage the application. Developers may also have a number of tools in place here to help with the monitoring of application performance and the capturing of exceptions.

Some of the tools in the run phase may be natively built into the platform you are using; some may be additional products and tools. For example, you may use the native monitoring capabilities in your cloud platform and then use an application performance monitoring tool to monitor both the infrastructure performance and the application performance.

From experience, this is one area of tooling that is lacking at many organizations; however, the right run tooling is critical to ensuring that you have the right technical feedback in terms of infrastructure and application performance so that you can make data-based decisions.

Now that we understand the different families of DevOps tools within the DevOps toolchain, let's now look at how tooling helps with the adoption of DevOps.

How does tooling help the adoption of DevOps?

DevOps uses its relationship to Agile development and then looks to create a culture that fosters collaboration and value streams. This is achieved by combining trusted principles and practices such as Lean, Theory of Constraints, and the Toyota Production System with Agile development.

In order to achieve this, DevOps requires an organization to adopt cultural changes within teams and adopt technical principles such as automation, version control, and continuous integration and delivery. In a similar way to the manufacturing industry, the integration of the right tools is fundamental to fully realize the benefits of the technical practices within DevOps.

A word of caution, though: DevOps is not just about using tools – it's about the combination of everything we have learned so far and interaction with tools that properly realizes the benefits of DevOps.

Here is a good set of guidelines that can be used to help pick the right tooling for your organization:

- Choose tools that facilitate collaboration.
- Use tools that enhance communication.
- Lean toward tools with APIs.
- Always encourage learning.
- Avoid environment-specific tools.

Now let's look at these guidelines in more detail to get a better understanding of how to apply them.

Choosing tools that facilitate collaboration

The ability to have effective collaboration between teams is critical for the success of DevOps. With tools specifically aimed at collaboration, it would be easy to think that you should buy a dedicated tool for this, but in the DevOps toolchain, there are lots of different tools you can use to enhance collaboration between teams.

A good example of this is version control, which is really a key element of the DevOps approach. As you are trying to encourage more people to make use of version control tools in the organizations, consider the impact of your tool choice. You and trusted members of your foundational team may be comfortable with a command line-only tool, but what about everyone else? Using a command line-only tool can end up as a barrier for some people who are more comfortable using user interfaces.

> **Important note**
> In this example, a command-line tool for version control is part of the DevOps toolchain but is unfamiliar to people, especially non-developers.

In this instance, there is very little collaboration opportunity given the limited audience of the command-line tool. However, if you adopt a version control platform such as GitLab, GitHub, BitBucket, or Azure DevOps, you can take advantage of discussion around file changes and commits within the code you are committing; this is a form of collaboration.

This helps collaboration with people who have different skills and encourages more people to learn how to use the platform for their own needs, thus helping to encourage collaboration.

The approach we discussed here works in other parts of the toolchain as well, not just for version control. It doesn't have to just impact a new tool either; this could be on existing tools within your organization.

Consider the impact of permissions on collaboration. A number of times, I have worked with operations teams who refuse to give developers access to what they believe is their tooling, thinking that nobody else should have access. If you want to improve collaboration, open that tool up to the developers – the result is better collaboration between the two teams. The tool has not changed, but the permissions have.

Using tools that enhance communication

In my experience, one of the biggest problems and certainly the most common problem among organizations building modern software platforms using a DevOps approach is the mismatch that exists between the responsibilities of teams and their tools.

Sometimes, organizations have multiple tools to achieve something when one tool would do the job. The reverse is also true: sometimes organizations have one single tool that causes problems when teams need separate tools.

One of the biggest impacts on the interaction between teams and the effectiveness of their communication is around the use of shared tools. Shared tools make sense to enable collaboration between teams, but if you need boundaries of responsibility to be clear, then using separate tools may be the best way to go. We discussed business benefits, team topologies, and the pitfalls of DevOps in *Chapter 2, Business Benefits, Team Topologies, and Pitfalls of DevOps*. Use this to understand which model is right for your organization.

If you are working toward a close working relationship between your development and operations teams, then a separate ticketing system will only result in poor communication between those teams. In order to help these teams be effective, you should choose a tool that meets the needs of both teams.

> Tip
> When considering tools, don't pick a tool for the whole organization before you have considered the team relationships first.

The key is to make sure you look at the whole organization, deploy tools that are shared for collaborative teams, and where you need to, don't be afraid to use separate tools.

Lean toward tools with APIs

Service-based architectures and API-driven applications are the cornerstones of cloud-native or cloud-ready systems. Tools that give you the ability to be customizable and highly automated are a major plus. Having tools that have full-featured APIs, and HTTP-based ones at that, are a must.

The use of APIs from a DevOps perspective allows you to take the many different tools you are using and connect them together as part of your processes. Tools that match these criteria are important, as when you come to change your existing tooling for something new, it is easy to change the plumbing that sticks everything together.

It is really easy to chain together tools using this method, but you need to be careful about scripts that are undocumented in this process. Tools that power the software delivery and operations processes should be treated like production tools. This means having the ability to properly document and release these tools.

Many organizations at the lower end of the maturity scale make the mistake of implementing new tools without the operational support needed to make those tools work well and be effective.

In summary, you should be aiming to gain new capabilities by combining multiple API-driven tools.

Always encouraging learning

When you look at the tools in the DevOps toolchain, quite a few of them are rather involved and can be very complicated, especially when people are new to the tooling. When tools are complex, you shouldn't expect everyone to adopt them quickly.

The opposite can also happen, in that when a tool is complicated and difficult to use, people may dig in their heels and not use it. This is why you have to think about providing training opportunities for people with new tools.

The introduction of a new tool requires you to assess the wider skills within your organization and then build a roadmap for the teams to move to improved ways of working. Giving people the opportunity to learn at their own pace is crucial, so looking at tools with multiple interfaces, such as a user interface, command line, and API, gives everyone the ability to learn.

The process of adopting DevOps is one of moving from manual to automated; not everyone will be in the same place at the same time, so giving people the ability and especially the space to learn gives you the best chance of people successfully adopting new tools and approaches.

Think of this as a step evolution: avoid fear by introducing tools that are scary and give people the option to learn at their own pace. Just like Agile teaches incremental improvement through sprints, treat your tooling the same and prefer those small gains over future state and a big bang approach.

Avoiding environment-specific tools

With the adoption of DevOps comes an increase in speed and frequency of delivery. This means that to be successful, you need to increase the feedback loops within your delivery and operations processes. As many technology-focused people as possible should be learning as much as they can about how production works so that, in turn, they can build more reliable products that are more resilient. Changes to the system should also be tested before any deployment to production.

Any tools that are only running in production cause problems because this prevents people from learning, as production is treated as a special case rather than just another environment your application runs in.

To be as effective as possible, you should choose tools that work in all environments; this even includes the developer's local environment in some cases. Watch out for tools that charge per environment to deploy or install and try to look for tools that provide site-wide license approaches to keep costs down if at all possible.

Think about the automation approach of DevOps as well; good DevOps tools should be able to be set up automatically in each environment. Stay away from tools that require manual effort to deploy – these tools are not good choices in DevOps.

When you run the same tool throughout each environment, you are increasing the level of engagement between your teams and increasing learning opportunities. Keeping a tool to production only locks people out of learning opportunities.

In summary, when it comes to environment-specific tools, avoid them at all costs. This breaks the feedback loop around learning, as well as making your continuous integration and delivery difficult.

Now we understand how tooling helps your adoption of DevOps, let's look at the benefits of DevOps tooling.

Understanding the benefits of DevOps tooling

According to the *State of DevOps report (2017)* by Puppet (`https://puppet.com/blog/2017-state-devops-report-here`), *"the ability to develop and deliver software efficiently and accurately is a key differentiator and value driver for all organizations."* While the report may be a few years old now, the content is still right on point when we talk about why we do DevOps.

The report finds that DevOps organizations are more than twice as likely to overachieve when it comes to efficiency, satisfaction, quality, and the fulfillment of organizational goals. Those objectives give a great insight into successful DevOps organizations. But how do they do it?

Using those key points as a benchmark, integrating the right tools to successfully apply DevOps technical practices will enable you to realize the following benefits:

- Increased code and deployment velocity

- Reduction of time to market for new products and features

- Decrease in the failure rate of new releases

- Improve the mean time to recovery

- Improvement in reliability metrics

- Enhanced collaboration and productivity

- Eliminating high levels of work in progress and technical debt

We have already explored the benefits of enhanced collaboration and productivity through some of the examples earlier in the chapter; one common theme between all of these benefits is around collaboration and communication, but let's now take a look at these benefits in more detail using tooling as examples.

Increasing code and deployment velocity

It's really not possible to accurately measure velocity around deployments and code without having tooling in place. A combination of information from your version control software, your backlog management tooling, and your pipeline environment will be needed to gain insights into this information.

Having this tooling in place and having the ability to accurately report on velocity is important: it helps you plan better as a team as well as understanding your limitations in terms of how much work you can complete in a single sprint.

Understanding this in the long term also helps you make decisions about when to hire more team members, especially when you combine this information with your technical debt and work in progress.

Reduction of time to market for new products and features

Communication and collaboration are really at the center of this one, especially at the start of this process. When you have good tools that foster good collaboration between teams, as well as good communication, you have the ability to take your ideas from inception to production quicker.

Add into that tooling around continuous integration and deployment, and all of a sudden, once your idea has been developed and tested, it can be deployed in no time at all, going through the various testing cycles.

This alone is a huge business driver for many organizations, especially those in the business of software. If you are able to take your ideas to market quicker than your competitors, this gives you a competitive edge over them, ultimately giving your customers more reasons to use your product over theirs.

Decrease in the failure rate of new releases

When you have invested in your pipelines to a point where they handle your deployments consistently, that brings into focus the need for a feedback loop. That loop, in this instance, is around improving the quality of the build and release pipelines.

By introducing the monitoring of your pipelines and using the built-in reporting that is in many existing CI and CD tools, you are able to pull metrics that show the success of your pipeline executions.

When a failure occurs, see this as a learning opportunity, pull information as to why it happened, and find out what you can do to improve quality so it does not happen again. This cycle, with the information you are gathering, goes to decrease the failure rate of your releases and helps you develop higher-quality pipelines.

Improving the mean time to resolution

Nobody likes downtime in their application, no matter how well the infrastructure is designed or how well the application is developed. You are likely to experience downtime at some point.

Monolithic environments or legacy working environments have traditionally had a harsh view on application downtime and the impact of that downtime. Today, instead of measuring **Service Level Agreements (SLAs)**, many organizations who practice DevOps are now turning to the measurement of **mean time to resolution (MTTR)**, which measures the mean average time to recover a service from a failure.

Site reliability tooling is critical in this space to enable you to gain as much information as possible about the outage. This includes 360-degree monitoring of your infrastructure and application, including performance and exceptions; user journeys; and synthetic transactions monitoring every aspect of the application's performance, availability, and security.

Important note

You should also not underestimate the importance of log files, which are often overlooked.

Log files add another dimension to your troubleshooting capabilities as well. So often, I have seen developers and operations teams scratching their heads because they don't have the appropriate logs available to diagnose an application outage.

When you have all this information at your disposal, as well as good communication, collaboration, and documentation, you stand a better chance of getting to the bottom of the issue as quickly as possible.

Measuring the endpoint availability of your application also gives you the ability to measure MTTR. You can measure the time between outage and the resumption of service. After each outage, it is important to sit back and review the information collected and look not only at how to avoid the outage again but also how to make process changes or changes anywhere else to reduce the amount of time needed to restore service next time.

Improvement in reliability metrics

Right off the back of MTTR is the improvement of reliability metrics. Using many of the same principles we discussed previously, you can also improve the reliability of all facets of your application.

The majority of site reliability and instrumentation tools will be able to feed into producing a dashboard or scorecard that gives you a picture of your reliability. As discussed previously, using this data to actually go forward and improve reliability is what sets organizations apart in levels of maturity.

Eliminating high levels of work in progress and technical debt

One of the biggest killers of productivity in a DevOps environment is the amount of work in progress and high levels of **technical debt** that exist at some organizations. All backlog management tools that I have worked with give you the ability to flag up via a dashboard or on a Kanban board, for example, the amount of work in progress for each team member.

Make sure the level of work here is acceptable. What is acceptable, of course, differs per team in general and of course per individual, their skills, and the work they are capable of completing.

Striking a balance can be difficult, but when people have too many "work in progress" items, it kills productivity. My experience tells me that each individual stays highly productive when they have no more than three active work in progress items. After this point, their productivity will start to take a tumble.

Another killer of productivity is the levels of technical debt in the organization. Technical debt, sometimes known as design debt, reflects the cost of additional rework in your application.

For example, if you designed a part of your application using an easy method today, instead of using a better approach that would take longer, that is technical debt. We usually then add technical debt to the backlog to revisit at a later date and resolve.

In order to understand your levels of technical debt, you need a reliable way of recording it. In some tools, you could create a specific backlog template to record it, or simply add a tag to a user story or bug – you decide how to record it.

You can then run queries and add data to dashboards to highlight your technical debt. When it gets to levels that you deem unacceptable, you can run a technical debt sprint aimed at reducing the amount of technical debt.

We have spent this section looking at the benefits of tooling in the DevOps toolchain and seeing how different tools add benefit to our DevOps value. Next, let's look at the obstacles that exist when it comes to onboarding successful tooling.

Understanding the obstacles of DevOps tooling

So far, we have covered all the positives about tooling in the DevOps toolchain. What about some of the obstacles that come from working with so many different tools? Here are a few things that are obstacles to the adoption of these tools:

- Lack of definition of DevOps
- Shortage of knowledge on tooling
- Evaluation of tools
- The volume of tools available on the market
- Lack of tool integration

Let's now look at these points in more detail to better understand the obstacles to adopting tools.

Lack of definition of DevOps outcomes

It goes without saying that without a properly defined definition of what DevOps is and what it means to your organization, you are going to struggle with tooling. This leads to organizations deploying tooling because their competitors are deploying tools or for other primitive reasons.

Having that definition also helps you understand what the tooling roadmap might look like and how you can properly address the gaps that exist with the right tools, using all the pointers we have discussed in this chapter.

Not only does your organization need a definition of DevOps, but it also needs to be standard across your whole organization. Everyone from top to bottom needs to buy into this in order for every part of your DevOps adoption to be successful; this includes tooling.

Inadequate knowledge of tooling

Having a shortage of knowledge on the different tooling available can also be a barrier to success. This issue can manifest in a few ways; however, some of them are more damaging to overall progress than others.

Firstly, a lack of knowledge can hamper your efforts to pick the right tool for the task. While nobody will ever be an expert in the whole toolchain, or even in one specific area, having broad knowledge will help you make an evaluation in line with the information you are able to gather from the vendor.

Secondly, the lack of knowledge can leave you in limbo – without that broad knowledge of the tooling, you may find yourself in a position where you don't understand how the tools are addressing your specific needs. This delay can hurt your implementation.

Thirdly, and finally, when you have a lack of tooling knowledge, the worst it can do is paralyze your decision making. Rather than making the wrong decision, as in point one, or lacking understanding, as in point two, this is more about misunderstanding what the tool is there to achieve.

Evaluation of tools

As with any purchase of software from any vendor, your organization is going to want to make sure you get the most from any demonstration or trial offers. This is a big investment, and you want to make sure you are picking a tool that checks the right boxes and delivers what you need.

Take into account the cost of a tool against the value it provides. You must make sure that the return on investment for the purchase is in line with expectations.

If you are evaluating multiple tools, make sure the evaluation of them is equal. There is no point performing different evaluations on tools that do the same thing. Not only does this not give each of your candidates the opportunity to shine, but it ensures that no bias is involved in the decision-making process.

Everyone has an affinity with different technology stacks and tools, but you need to make sure you pick the right tool for the organization, not use what you have used in the past just because you know the tool.

The volume of tools available on the market

Of course, before you even get to the evaluation of tools, you have to tread your way through the vast ocean of tools that exist in the various categories of the DevOps toolchain.

The number of tools is so vast that the **Cloud Native Computing Foundation (CNCF)** has even created a web tool detailing the tools within their area and provides a number of filters for you to limit your searches. This is the *CNCF Cloud Native Landscape* (`https://landscape.cncf.io`). Don't be mistaken: this is incredibly useful, but it also highlights the issues we face when selecting tools.

To add to the list of tools charted by the CNCF, there are of course other tools as well that are not within the CNCF ecosystem. This expansive list of tools adds to the paralysis you can feel when looking at the tooling options available.

You can get through the marketing offered by the vendors by looking at independent sources of information on the tools. Go to community posts by people who use the products, look at their use cases, and use this information to help you shortlist tools.

Lack of tool integration

Earlier in the chapter, we talked about the importance of integration within DevOps tooling. Working with a tool that lacks sufficient integration limits your capability, depending on that limitation depends on the impact it has.

For example, continuous integration and deployment tooling without sufficient integration is going to be a problem if the platform doesn't provide a wide array of other services with it. When looking at these tools, we should look for integration opportunities with backlog management tools, our deployment platform, and our ticketing system if that is a requirement.

We also must consider integration with tools providing security services for them to be valuable to our overall ambitions.

That lack of integration creates a black box for your tooling, where you are unable to interface with it or retrieve what might be valuable data from it.

Summary

In this chapter, we have looked at tooling within the DevOps toolchain. We have looked at the different families of DevOps tooling and looked at how tooling helps the adoption of DevOps in your organization. We then looked at the benefits of DevOps tooling and looked to understand the obstacles that may prevent the adoption of good-quality tools.

Next, we will look at how to develop a strategy for the implementation of tooling. We will look at the architectural and security requirements for your tooling and how to develop training plans to help the team, and tie this in with defining owners and processes for DevOps tools.

Questions

Let's now recap some of what we have learned throughout this chapter:

1. Which tools have an impact across the whole DevOps toolchain?

   a. Build tools

   b. Testing tools

   c. Collaboration tools

   d. Run tools

2. Why are APIs so important when adopting tooling?

   a. They're not – we don't need APIs.

   b. They provide automation and integration opportunities.

   c. DevOps engineers need to learn about APIs.

   d. All good tools come with APIs anyway.

10
Developing a Strategy for Implementing Tooling

Simply picking tooling and implementing it in your environment is not going to make you successful and will set your DevOps transformation back. You should engage others, listen to concerns, and develop a strategy for implementing your tooling. In this chapter, we will look at the considerations for creating a strategy for tooling.

By the end of this chapter, you will understand the importance of following architectural best practices as well as security requirements at all times, learn how to develop training plans to help your team use the new tooling, and learn about the importance of having owners and processes associated with tooling.

In this chapter, we're going to cover the following main topics:

- Understanding architectural and security requirements
- Developing training plans to help your team
- Defining owners and processes for tooling

Understanding architectural and security requirements

When you're implementing anything in your organization, be that new tools or even technical processes or updates to existing tools, it is important to consider the impact this will have on the enterprise architecture and information security. These two groups are the cornerstone of IT organizations and working toward their defined goals, which will closely align with the business goals, will help you in your search for appropriate tooling.

To explore this further, it's important to understand the following:

- Why is enterprise architecture important?
- Why is information security important?
- Understanding architectural requirements
- Understanding security requirements

Let's look at these four points in more detail to get a better understanding.

Why is enterprise architecture important?

There are many benefits to **enterprise architecture** within an organization. The most obvious is the top-down view of systems within the enterprise. This alone makes enterprise architecture invaluable when it comes to managing the complexities involved with many businesses.

In years gone by, many people saw enterprise architecture as a sole function of IT and operating from the ivory tower. In recent years, this view has changed dramatically. Instead of enterprise architecture just being thought of as a function of IT, it now plays a pivotal role in bridging the gap that exists between the business and IT.

The practice of enterprise architecture has evolved over the years. From being a foundational and supporting role, it is now more progressive and outcome-focused and identifies opportunities for change and growth.

Enterprise architecture is important because it determines the overall strategy for services and applications. A strategy and roadmap for enterprise architecture will define blueprints for deploying services, a list of things services must have before they will be considered for service. It also defines the platforms that the organization will use in the short, mid, and long term.

Therefore, taking all this information into account when you are looking at tooling around DevOps means that you have a lot to consider. Does your tooling meet the requirements that have been set out for applications that your organization will use?

When I think about enterprise architecture, I think of three main benefits that it provides to an organization:

- Management of complexity
- Creating actionable deliverables
- Increasing agility and reducing time to value

Let's look at these three areas in more detail.

Management of complexity

Most organizations, especially enterprises, are a mesh of systems and applications. That mesh has a variety of degrees of importance and prominence within the organization. There are no real rules to defining these degrees of importance or prominence either. That is part of what makes it complex.

Some applications are incredibly important to the success of the business, but outside of IT, people may not know what the application is called.

> **Important Note**
> The top-down view that enterprise architectures use means that organizations are more efficient and confident at assessing assets such as applications.

The holistic view that enterprise architecture brings is there to build up not just one area, but areas across the whole organization. This provides views that, for example, might identify areas where multiple applications are addressing the same process.

Another view may conclude that an application that is seemingly less prominent is actually integral. That view helps us avoid scenarios where leadership might be thinking about phasing the application out from the landscape.

Creating actionable deliverables

Previously, we talked about assessing our current capabilities and managing the complex landscape that is in many organizations. With the holistic view we discussed, this also helps enterprise architecture teams identify any gaps.

This all-round better understanding of the architecture within an organization means that organizations can make more informed decisions, including *what* they should invest in going forward.

Importantly, it also helps the organization understand *when* roadmaps can be created so that they can reflect on an organization's key priorities, and pressing concerns throughout the organization can impact this.

Overall, this approach will help the organization meet the current demands that have been placed on it, as well as current opportunities. All of this happens while mitigating any disruption to service. It ensures this can be done with the long-term vision of the organization.

Increasing agility and reducing time to value

Today, in the era of rapidly evolving technology, as well as often highly disruptive digital transformation, the need for tools to help with enterprise architecture is clear.

Tools will help speed up the decision support for optimization, alternative investment, rationalization, and planning for risks, change, and the overall impact to the organization. Organizations that translate all of this into tangible outputs are better equipped to evaluate as well as implement new technology in an efficient manner.

In short, a well-functioning enterprise architecture will help the business capture and understand, as well as articulate, the opportunities, risks, and challenges that exist. This includes security. Let's look at the importance of information security.

Why is information security important?

In the modern world, where data is king and most of our data is stored in systems, information security is incredibly important. Mishaps in data handling and security incidents can sink companies and cause irreparable damage to an organization's reputation.

Sadly, many people still have no idea about how important information security is to a business and, of course, the success of that business. Many managers also still hold the frightening misconception that information being controlled by them is secure and free from threat. This misconception is, of course, a big mistake.

In our roles as technologists today, we enjoy the benefits of years of advancement in the technology we use. Because of this, cyber-attacks are on the rise and increasingly more damaging. Repeat attacks are on the rise and before you realize it, your organization could be the target of another cyber-attack and already at risk.

This is why you have to be very careful when it comes to handling and processing confidential pieces of information.

Why should my organization worry about security?

Consider the importance of internal information about your organization. Strategy plans, financial information, employee records, merger and acquisition information – the list is endless.

If leaked, this has a serious domino effect, which quickly triggers several other consequences, such as damaging your reputation, exposing your strategy, and exposing any company secrets or intellectual property.

Not only can this information be damaging to your company, but what about your customers? You likely hold information about your customers, such as who they are, what they use, how much they spend, what they spend it on, and maybe even their plans for the future, which is now freely available on the internet.

Outside of the enterprise, many smaller organizations think they are not targets for cyber criminals and do not need to invest in data security and cyber defenses.

In fact, due to this lack of protection, many successful attacks target companies of this size; many don't know that their systems have even been compromised until well after the event, when it's too late.

I recommend watching this video on *YouTube* (`https://www.youtube.com/watch?v=7L9JerWIT3Y`) about the importance of information security. The video looks at where sensitive information is stored and the various types of information we handle to explain the importance of information security.

Which common threats should I be aware of?

Tools exist to deal with common threats. Code scanning tools in particular will look for vulnerability exploits within the source code of an application. Threats are dealt with by information security professionals on a daily basis. From my experience, I would say that the following five threats are the most common ones that professionals have to deal with:

- Exploiting vulnerabilities
- Malware

- Phishing
- Systems offline
- Lack of confidentiality

Let's have a look at these five threats in more detail.

Exploiting vulnerabilities

Hackers and cyber criminals look for vulnerabilities within systems that can help facilitate their attacks. Typically, vulnerabilities exist because of negligence in the management of those systems, such as not changing passwords and not updating those systems to include the latest vendor updates.

Sometimes though, hackers take advantage of what are called zero-day vulnerabilities, which have not yet had a patch released by the vendor.

Malware

One of the most common vectors of attack that goes back to the beginning of cyber-attacks is malware. Simply put, malware is an infectious agent that attacks software of part of an application with malicious code. The purpose of this is to damage data or even devices within the organization.

A more extreme example of this is the SolarWinds Orion attack in 2020. This was an attack fundamentally on the supply chain, where malicious code was inserted during the build and release process. This method ensures that, if undetected, your malware is in the final product and the binaries of the software are signed, making them look like genuine releases.

Updates were then applied to the product as part of regular maintenance and organizations around the world unknowingly installed software with a backdoor onto their networks.

Other examples of malware in the form of a supply chain attack include the Target security breach, as well as the Stuxnet virus, which targeted control and data acquisition systems, according to *Business Insider* (`https://www.businessinsider.com/ stuxnet-was-far-more-dangerous-than-previous-thought-2013-11`), rendering 1/5th of Iran's nuclear centrifuges damaged.

Phishing

The rise of phishing is huge. The root of phishing attacks is electronic fraud. One of the ways criminals act is via impersonation. This could be by faking emails from someone trusted within your organization, enticing you to click links in emails that are actually infected.

In the outside world, the biggest goals of phishing are to steal banking information, as well as identities. In the corporate world, though, this includes information about your business and what you plan to do with it.

Systems offline

One of the most common attacks over the past 10 years is the denial of service attack. Most organizations have business-critical systems that cannot be unavailable. The denial of service attack looks at targeting these critical systems with so many requests that the application is unable to handle the volume of requests and crashes.

These incidents are extremely serious and can lead to loss of revenue for organizations, as well as damaging their reputation and customer confidence.

Lack of confidentiality

Most organizations handle a level of sensitive information, some more sensitive than others. The majority of organizations handle personal data, even if that is just about employees.

Some data, including personal data, should be protected and made accessible only by people who are authorized to access that data and are reliable. Many organizations spend large amounts of money before employees start performing background checks to ensure they are reliable individuals.

The basic rule of information protection is that when this rule of access and trust is not followed, people outside the circle of trust for that data may have access to that data and be able to misuse it.

To conclude, information security is incredibly important, and awareness within your organization about who is responsible is also incredibly important. It's quite simple: everyone is responsible for security within your organization; it is the job of the security professionals to hunt, detect, and track down individuals who try and break trust and attempt to infiltrate your networks.

Now, let's look at the importance of understanding architectural requirements when developing a strategy for tooling.

Understanding architectural requirements

Now that we have a solid understanding of enterprise architecture and the role it plays in our organization, let's look at how can we use that to help build a strategy that helps with our tooling choices later down the line.

Defining our architectural requirements

First of all, let's define some architectural requirements we can use to align to tooling choices in the DevOps space. Our first requirement is that, where possible, we will buy software as opposed to building it ourselves. Next up is that the system must be able to accept our federated corporate identities. This means support for technology such as OAuth or **Security Assertion Markup Language** (**SAML**) so that we can use single sign-on.

OAuth is an open standard for access delegation that is commonly used by internet users to grant websites or applications access to their information on other websites, without revealing their passwords. On the other hand, SAML is an open standard that allows identity providers to pass authorization credentials to service providers.

Other requirements include that the software must be able to be deployed to a public cloud provider, and that we must be able to interface with the tool using an API.

To summarize, this is our shortlist of requirements:

- Buy software over building it internally.
- Accept federated identity.
- Support deploying to a public cloud provider.
- Interface using an API.

In the real world, many more requirements will be defined, and are set out by enterprise architecture. These requirements help us navigate the choices of tools on the market and naturally help us narrow down our choices.

Preparing for architecture reviews

Mature organizations that practice enterprise architecture will also set out the requirement for all new projects to go before a board. This is composed of leaders from parts of the business and is run by enterprise architecture.

The goal of this board, often called the Architecture Review Board, is to ensure that new software coming into the organization has met the criteria of the enterprise architecture blueprint and can address any additional questions that may come up.

When you are going through the process of looking at options for tooling, have a member of the enterprise architecture team work with you on it. That way, many of the questions that will be asked at the review board will be asked during your time evaluating tools.

Overall, this could save you a significant amount of time. Now that we have looked at the importance of architectural and security requirements regarding tooling within your organization, let's look at how you can develop training plans to help your teams adopt new tools.

Developing training plans to help your team

Often, organizations do not put enough of an emphasis on the requirement for teams to be trained on new tools that are brought into the organization. Training comes in many forms, and you will need to make sure that you cater your training for different teams if multiple teams use your tool and to suit people's styles of learning.

Considering these things up front, and then putting a plan in place around them, is likely to make your tooling implementation more successful than it would have been without appropriate training plans.

Now, let's look at the importance of developing training plans within your organization.

Why are training plans important?

Let's take a professional sportsperson as an example. Their training is fundamentally important to their success. As the training process for professional athletes becomes more detailed, variances arise in their training, such as planning the weather all the way through to preparing for major events. A plan is needed to give you structure, direction, and guidance. Training plans also help you prepare and deal with different factors, such as distractions that can interfere with the plan.

> **Important Note**
> Training plans help you plan ahead, increase staff retention, and increase engagement, as well as helping you stay ahead of competitors.

Training plans are important in businesses for a number of reasons, but here are a few from the top of my head:

- Increasing employee engagement
- Improving staff retention
- Staying ahead of your competitors
- Saving on costs

Let's look at these reasons in more detail to look at why training plans are important.

Increasing employee engagement

Lack of engagement ultimately leads to issues in retention (more on that next). Keeping your team engaged, especially as a group of technical people, involves training that helps them further their careers.

If your organization has a good track record of providing quality training opportunities, then your employees stay engaged. They know that when something new comes along, they will get the opportunity to learn.

Improving staff retention

Anyone who has spent time managing a team knows that it's inevitable that, in time, one of your team members is going to raise points such as, "I don't know where my career is going" or "I don't think the company values what I do." While comments like these may not be an immediate problem, they lead to people looking at other jobs, which leads to interviews, and then offers.

Planning ahead, and then communicating those training plans so that your team knows how their training over that period will be aligned with your organization's objectives, helps them put things into perspective.

Staying ahead of your competitors

Objectives are usually built around growth, market share, delivering products and services, or increasing sales. You can still attach training goals to those objectives, and your training plan should reflect those goals.

Design what your teams need to know in advance; that is, what they need to make them and you successful. When you get to that critical point where that knowledge or those skills are needed, your successful training plans mean that employees already have those skills.

Saving on costs

Doesn't everyone like to save money? As a summary, really, when you are recruiting, you can bring someone in with all the knowledge you need as opposed to someone internal who acquires that knowledge over time. It is cheaper for someone to acquire that knowledge than it is to hire someone who knows it.

Planning will help you spend your training budget more efficiently. You can plan in advance for what you need and when and use people internally where you can, but in short, when it comes to developing your team, planning is always key.

Now, let's look at how you can develop training plans for teams in your organization.

How to develop training plans for your teams

Developing training plans is actually a fairly well-defined process. Training plans should just be a part of your entire organization's training program, which should be in place already.

Developing an effective plan involves the following steps:

1. Identify the training needs
2. Review the adult learning principles
3. Develop objectives for the individual
4. Design or seek out appropriate training
5. Plan when the training will take place
6. Have employees sign off on the plan

Let's look at these steps in more detail to understand how we can develop training plans.

Identify the training needs

You should consider the differences in teams using tools. If multiple teams are using the tool, then not every team will be using the tool in the same way. Before developing your plan, perform an audit of existing skills, and then work out what you and your employees need before you start planning.

If you develop a plan that does not provide any value, people will not be engaged and won't see the value, no matter how hard you try.

Review the adult learning principles

It sounds obvious, but bear in mind that adults learn differently from children. Your training plan needs to reflect this. You need to make sure training will keep people engaged; don't plan training that just runs through PowerPoint slides.

Most adults learn by self-directing, and the choices they make are relevant to their personal objectives. Adult learning is also heavily goal-oriented, so make sure your training is aligned with the objectives of the business, both personally and professionally.

The life experience that's gained by adults when it comes to training is also important, as this experience can help shape their future training. These previous experiences help determine your preferred learning style.

Develop objectives for the individual

Developing objectives with your training plans is important because if you don't, you don't know exactly where you want to go, and the training probably won't work. Having a final end goal is a start, but you need milestones along the way to make sure you are heading in the right direction.

Learning objectives should fundamentally define what you want employees to understand and, most importantly, be able to do at the end of the training process. At the end of training, employees should know what they can do now that they couldn't before they took on the training.

Design or seek out appropriate training

Try and look internally for a subject expert that may be able to help you deliver any training. Failing that, you may be able to find suitable material you can use already on the internet. In other instances, you may need to have a trainer come in and help train your employees.

During this step, consider the learning styles of employees and how that might affect what you class as appropriate training.

Separate training so that there is a clear definition between your soft skills and hard skills. Hard skills would be classed as technical skills in a new product or tool, while soft skills would be things such as communication, diversity, or harassment training.

Plan when the training will take place

As a manager, make sure your team is fully aware that they have dedicated learning time available to take training as required. You should actively encourage your employees to make use of the time that's been set aside for them and make commitments so that when training is booked in, it will not be moved. Often, training is one of the first things to get postponed or moved around due to operational challenges. Do what you can to ensure this is not the case.

You should use a tool or even just a spreadsheet to track the training that people have signed up for, completed, and intend to take.

Have employees sign off on the plan

Keep track of your training program and ensure that all your employees have completed the necessary modules. You can implement a training program that begins as soon as new employees are hired that focuses on health and safety, company culture, and general procedures. It is critical to obtain feedback from employees who have completed a specific program and for them to sign off on their training.

Now that you understand why training plans are important and how to develop and implement them in your organization, let's look at defining owners and processes for your tooling.

Defining owners and processes for tooling

For tooling to be effective, it really needs two fundamental things. The first is an owner for that tool, while the second is for processes to be defined and documented for that tool.

The owners of your tooling are responsible for defining how the tool is used, what scenarios it helps resolve, defining processes for how to use parts of the tool, and providing ownership in terms of the infrastructure and any costs behind it. You may split tool ownership between business ownership to manage the costs, infrastructure required, or license costs and a technical owner who looks after the knowledge articles and processes for how to use the tool.

Considerations should be made regarding the tool's life cycle at this point as well. While talking about test tooling, the following article from *Cania Consulting* (`https://cania-consulting.com/2019/10/25/software-testing-tool-basics/#Testing_tool_life_cycle`) provides a good explanation of the tool's life cycle.

Now, let's look at how to identify the owners of tools within your organization.

Identifying the owners of tools in your organization

If your organization is lucky enough to have an asset management team, then most of the business ownership may fall with them for any tooling that you bring in. License ownership would generally sit with asset management as a centralized team.

Technical ownership is not as clear as you might think. Sure, if one team uses a tool, then the ownership of that tool from a day-to-day perspective would sit with that team. Consider a scenario where the tool is more foundational and is used by many different teams.

In that scenario, you will find that the ownership of the tool generally sits with the central IT teams. In many organizations, this would traditionally be true, but with the adoption of DevOps tooling and the transformations going on within teams, many central IT teams are reluctant to own and manage tools they don't use.

In this scenario, central IT teams will provide underlying support for the tool if required, though this won't be needed in scenarios where the tool is PaaS or SaaS. The teams using the application daily will then be granted ownership of the application and assume those responsibilities.

Mapping processes to tools

Consider the processes that are needed to successfully operate your tool. You will need to think about traditional processes such as how users are onboarded to your tool and how their access and permissions are managed, all the way to how you remove people from the tool.

In addition, think about what problem the tool is trying to solve and the manual processes that it will automate. They need to be documented in detail so that if the automation process fails, people know what it's replacing and where to look to fix a problem.

Other processes you will need to think about include documenting the importance of the tool. This helps build up a picture of what the tool supports and how fundamental it is to the business. Also, think about how the tool should be updated and when it is used so that when it is updated, the service is not taken out for other important processes.

Making tooling part of process improvement

We have spoken about the importance of continuous feedback and continuous improvement several times now. Tooling should not be exempt from this cycle. It is as important to include your tooling in process improvement activities as it is the process.

Look at your processes that use value stream mapping; for example, it could be that the tooling is causing a delay or lead time in the process that you are trying to fix. In that context, you may need to make adjustments to the tooling for it to work correctly.

Summary

In this chapter, we understood the architectural and security requirements that need to be considered when looking at a tooling strategy. We also looked at why enterprise architecture and information security are important, how to develop training plans for your organizations, and how to identify owners and processes for your tooling.

Using these skills, you can now implement a strategy and process for DevOps tooling in your organization, as well as developing solid training plans that will allow your teams to get up to speed with the new tools.

In the next chapter, we'll look at the various trends that are closely aligned with DevOps, such as DataOps, DevSecOps, and GitOps. We will look at what they are and the tools that help deliver value in those XOps scenarios.

Questions

Now, let's recap what we have learned throughout this chapter:

1. Which one of these is not a reason why enterprise architecture is important?

    a. Management of complexity

    b. Dictating what tools should be used

    c. Creating actionable deliverables

    d. Increasing agility

2. Which of these steps is not part of developing a training plan?

    a. Developing objectives

    b. Saving money on training

    c. Planning for the training taking place

    d. Having employees sign off on the plan

11
Keeping Up with Key DevOps Trends

A number of different disciplines now exist that look to build upon the core principles and practices of DevOps and target different areas of the business, and even specific departments. Terms such as DataOps, GitOps, and DevSecOps are now common terminology in the industry and tooling exists for each of these, too. In this chapter, we look at some of these trends in more detail to understand what they are, what their goal is, and what tooling can be used.

By the end of this chapter, you will understand some of the key trends associated with DevOps specialties, understand what they are, how they apply to organizations, and how tooling can be used within them.

In this chapter, we're going to cover the following topics:

- What is XOps?
- Understanding the DataOps ecosystem
- Understanding the DevSecOps ecosystem
- Understanding the GitOps ecosystem

What is XOps?

XOps is a general catch-all term that describes the adoption of other forms of operations both inside and outside of technology. In this context, DevOps is really just the tip of the iceberg.

DevOps is just the beginning. You can also include BizOps, FinOps, AIOps, and MarketingOps as a start, but the term *XOps* covers more than just the ones listed here. These are all cross-functional efforts, like DevOps is, but do organizations really need all of them, even some of them, or is the movement just hype?

One thing we can all agree on is that all organizations are at their own stages of maturity. The factors for this include their size, age, industry, technical adoption, budgets, and, of course, culture.

Organizations are increasingly requiring the benefits of what these different kinds of operation models provide. Some organizations will implement as many of them as possible, while some will implement what they need and even manipulate the processes and level of adoption to best fit with their organization.

This does not mean that the results will be any different depending on the factors previously mentioned. As with DevOps, the key element that all of these models have in common is the focus on value, which is something unique to each organization.

Where did XOps begin?

Some people believe that XOps is just hype, hype that will disappear, and that much of what is proposed is a relabeling of what already exists. You can say the same about DevOps as well, but it is the way that practices within DevOps are brought together and not left fragmented that delivers real value to organizations.

Like DevOps, most of the types of operation models will look at the acceleration of the process and improvements in quality when it comes to what they deliver. For example, in DataOps, this would be data, and analytical insights into operations performance for AIOps.

Those who believe that XOps is overhyped believe that the risk is that fragmentation is created by the different groups that are involved. This fragmentation further dilutes the faster value that is created and creates a level of additional bureaucracy.

> **Important note**
> Agility has been at the heart of XOps since the turn of the millennium. Business leaders have since been aware that their organizations need to be more Agile in order to stay competitive in their industry.

Agile practices that form part of XOps have been around for some time and have been rising further up the business stack for some time. Sadly, some leaders take the view that agility will equal the ability to do more with less.

The truth is that fundamentally, agility backed up with solid processes provides your organization with the ability to scale when needed, deliver more value to your end users, improve your processes, and your efficiency.

The link between XOps and DevOps is not just in the similarities in names, approaches to achieving the gold standard, or the processes involved. Culture is an important part of DevOps, specifically regarding the ability to improve your communication and collaboration in your organization.

Other important aspects that XOps takes from DevOps is the focus on continuous improvement, as well as the focus on the automation of tasks. Technical staff often forget that process automation does not just have to be on technical elements of the process. After all, business process automation was around long before DevOps was conceived.

Understanding the XOps landscape

To understand the XOps landscape further, let's look at two of the common initiatives in XOps, which are FinOps and CloudOps. We will learn about DataOps, DevSecOps, and GitOps in more detail later in this chapter.

FinOps

FinOps is also known as Cloud Financial Management, and it is the amalgamation of finance and operations teams within an organization. Specifically, FinOps focuses on the processes involved in managing financial operations while linking together the people involved, the processes, and, of course, the technology.

The need for FinOps arises from the traditional financial model in IT, which worked separately from other teams and lacked a level of data-driven decision making and technical modernization for managing scalable, cloud-enabled applications.

Limitations regarding the lack of flexibility concerning business requirements only inflated the costs, which make the system slow moving and more expensive. As a result of this, organizations needed to come up with a method for providing cost control for their highly scalable cloud environments, understand what those costs are, how they are occurring, and keep track of their cloud spend.

As the cloud has evolved, so has the need for the ability to provide chargeback of services hosted in cloud environments for other parts of the organization. The granular costs involved with cloud computing have made the idea of chargeback simpler in many ways, but it is actually hard to implement.

Complexities around how to bill for shared services such as network and storage make it difficult to realize how these costs can be charged back to various departments. These fabric-level services, or core services, are often consumed by the technology department, while application services are charged back to cost centers.

To have robust practices regarding FinOps, it is important to follow three phases of adoption. These phases are inform, optimize, and operate. The first phase, *inform*, looks at a detailed assessment of assets, budget allocation, and providing an understanding of industry standards to detect areas of improvement.

The second phase, *optimize*, helps to set alerts and metrics that identify any areas that need to both spend and redistribute resources. These generate decision-making capabilities and provide recommendations on architecture changes where required.

The final phase, *operate*, assists in tracking costs and cost control mechanisms at a resource level. FinOps provides a level of flexibility in operations, but maintains financial accountability to the variable costs that are associated with cloud platforms.

CloudOps

CloudOps is the process of defining and identifying operational procedures, which are appropriate to optimizing services within cloud environments. CloudOps is a bringing together of DevOps and traditional operations allowing cloud platforms, applications, and data to provide further technical strengthening while maintaining services.

For organizations to accelerate agility any further, they must keep a check on any budget constraints, such as waste and overrun. This is one of the reasons why organizations decide to move to cloud platforms for their workloads.

CloudOps provides predictability and proactiveness and helps enhance visibility and governance. In maintaining on-premises locations, the associated power, network, storage, and high availability are always a challenge. This is easier in the cloud even though challenges remain, but those challenges differ from on-premises.

Since CloudOps is an extension of DevOps, it aims to build cloud operations teams that are responsible for post-migration applications on cloud platforms. Governance tools that optimize costs, enhance security posture, and provide capacity planning are essential in CloudOps. It also promotes the notion of continuous monitoring as well as the management of cloud applications with smaller numbers of resources.

Automation provides techniques to increase the agility, speed, and performance of cloud applications. Automation in CloudOps also facilitates the handling of services, incidents, and problems in a smooth manner. Combining elements of DevOps such as continuous integration and continuous deployment with infrastructure services and introducing infrastructure as code provides high levels of automation, increases the value of CloudOps, and provides level scalability not previously seen by operations teams.

Approach to XOps

Let's look at an example approach to XOps. The objective is to transform what is currently a monolithic application into a microservice architecture. Additionally, the migration process should be automated, along with separate environments for production, UAT, and test.

The primary identity should be managed by the DevOps team. This allows you to manage users and groups as well as third-party services and applications. This approach advocates collaborative culture.

Furthermore, to make resources modular, the team generates container-based modules for multiple resources, and stacks are then broken down, making them scalable and ensuring that deployment is easier.

Maintenance and debugging with this approach become simpler for development teams as well, and automated processes help enhance code quality. Role-based access control ensures secure authentication and authorization.

The deployment of centralized systems for logging and monitoring allows views of performance, availability, and security on centralized dashboards. This helps to provide cost-effectiveness and improve the performance of the application.

Here, we have discussed a number of disciplines, such as DevOps, CloudOps, and FinOps, to make this happen.

We now have an understanding of the term *XOps*. We understand where XOps came from and the landscape of XOps. Let's now look at the DataOps ecosystem in more detail.

Understanding the DataOps ecosystem

One of the most common misconceptions around DataOps is that under the covers, it is just DevOps applied to data analytics. While the name shares similarities with both DevOps and DataOps, they're not the same.

Look at the following diagram, which depicts the DevOps loop:

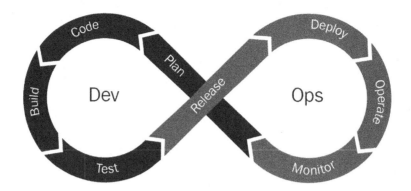

Figure 11.1 – Graphic showing the phases of DevOps in an infinite loop

DevOps is often depicted as an infinite loop. As you can see in the previous diagram, DataOps is different. When illustrating DataOps, it is shown as an intersection of value and innovation pipelines, as you can see in the following diagram:

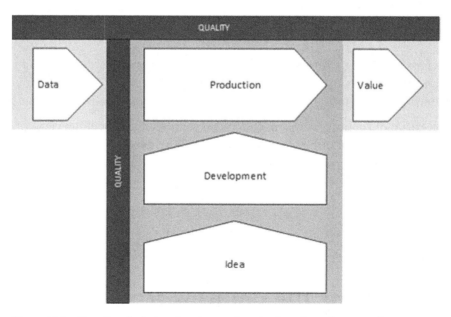

Figure 11.2 – DataOps depiction showing a value pipeline along the top and innovation from bottom to top

DataOps communicates that data analytics can achieve what DevOps accomplished for software development. That is, when data teams use new tools and methodologies, DataOps can result in an order of magnitude improvement in quality and cycle time. The specific methods by which DataOps achieves these gains reflect the distinct people, processes, and tools that characterize data teams.

The Agile methodology is particularly useful in environments where requirements evolve quickly and often change. This is a situation that data professionals will understand all too well. Like in DevOps, Agile in DataOps allows organizations to respond very quickly to requirements and accelerate the time to value.

DataOps is also as much about managing people as it is about the tools. The needs and preferences of stakeholders are one subtle difference between DataOps and DevOps.

In DevOps, our users are software engineers and operations engineers who are comfortable with coding, the complexity involved with multiple languages in one environment, as well as hardware and software. However, in DataOps, our users are data scientists, engineers, and analysts who analyze data and build complex data models.

DevOps was developed to meet the needs of software developers. Dev engineers enjoy coding and are technologically savvy. Learning a new language or deploying a new tool is an opportunity, not a burden. They take a keen interest in all aspects of code creation, integration, and deployment. DevOps welcomes complexity.

DataOps users are frequently the polar opposite of that. They are data scientists or analysts who specialize in the development and deployment of models and visualizations. Engineers are typically more technically savvy than scientists and analysts. They concentrate on domain expertise. They are interested in making models more predictive or determining the best way to visually render data.

The technology used to create these models and visualizations is merely a tool. Data professionals are happiest when they only use one or two tools. Anything more adds unwelcome complexity. In the most extreme cases, the complexity exceeds their ability to manage it.

DataOps recognizes that data professionals live in a multi-tool, heterogeneous world, and strives to make it more manageable for them.

Understanding processes involved in DataOps

By examining data analytics development and life cycle processes, we can begin to understand the unique complexity that data professionals face. We discovered that data analytics professionals face challenges that are both similar to and distinct from those faced by software developers.

In DevOps, the life cycle starts with the planning phase, and this feeds back to the beginning, which is the code phase. Hence, the process iterates indefinitely.

The DataOps life cycle shares these iterative characteristics, but there is a significant difference: DataOps consists of two active and intersecting pipelines. The previously mentioned data factory is a single pipeline. The other pipeline governs how the data factory is updated, which includes the creation and deployment of new analytics into the data pipeline.

The process by which new analytic ideas are introduced into the value pipeline is referred to as the innovation pipeline. Although the innovation pipeline conceptually resembles the DevOps development process, several factors make the DataOps development process more difficult than DevOps.

Understanding tools involved in DataOps

To deliver a reliable data pipeline, the tooling to directly and indirectly support DataOps needs can be broken down into five steps, leveraging existing analytics tools along with toolchain components meant to address source control management, process management, and efficient communication among groups:

- Source control management

- Automation of processes and workflow

- Adding data and logic tests

- Working without fear with consistent deployment

- Implementing communication and process management

Now, let's provide a little more detail regarding these five steps.

Source control management

A data pipeline is nothing more than source code that is responsible for converting raw data into usable information. We can automate the data pipeline from start to finish, resulting in reproducible source code. A revision control tool (such as GitHub) aids in the storage and management of all changes to code and configuration in order to reduce inconsistent deployment.

Automation of processes and workflow

Automation is essential for the success of the DataOps methodology, which necessitates the design of a data pipeline with runtime flexibility. Automated data curation services, metadata management, data governance, master data management, and self-service interaction are critical requirements for achieving this.

Adding data and logic tests

To ensure that the data pipeline is working properly, inputs, outputs, and business logic must be tested. To ensure consistent data quality, the data pipeline is tested at each stage for accuracy or potential deviation, as well as errors or warnings.

Working without fear with consistent deployment

Data analytics professionals are terrified of introducing changes that will disrupt the current data pipeline. This can be addressed with two key workflows that will be integrated later in production. For starters, the value pipeline generates ongoing value for organizations. Second, the innovation pipeline consists of new analytics in the development stage that are later added to the production pipeline.

Implementing communication and process management

Within a DataOps practice, efficient and automated notifications are critical. When changes are made to any source code, or a data pipeline is triggered, failed, completed, or deployed, the appropriate stakeholders can be immediately notified. The toolchain also includes tools for facilitating cross-stakeholder communication (think Slack or Trello).

We now have an understanding of what DataOps is, what it tries to achieve when implemented correctly, as well as an understanding of the processes and tooling involved in the DataOps life cycle. Now, let's look at the DevSecOps ecosystem.

Understanding the DevSecOps ecosystem

DevSecOps is a software industry culture shift that aims to incorporate security into the rapid-release cycles typical of modern application development and deployment, also known as the DevOps movement. Embracing this shift-left mindset necessitates organizations bridging the gap that typically exists between development and security teams, to the point where many of the security processes are automated and handled by engineering teams.

The following diagram helps depict how security fits into the existing DevOps loop:

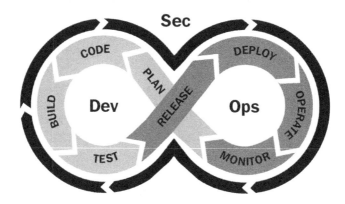

Figure 11.3 – Diagram showing the interaction between DevOps and DevSecOps

Historically, major software developers would release new versions of their applications every few months, if not years. This gave the code enough time to go through quality assurance and security testing, which was handled by separate specialized teams, either internal or externally contracted.

However, the last 10 years have seen a rise in public clouds, containers, and the microservice model, which divides monolithic applications into smaller parts that run independently. This breakdown has also had a direct impact on the way software is developed, resulting in rolling releases and Agile development practices in which new features and code are constantly pushed into production at a rapid pace.

DevSecOps combines DevOps and SecOps to form a cyclical practice for software development, technology operations, and cybersecurity.

DevSecOps aims to promote the rapid development of a secure code base. Rather than emphasizing development speed or security, the DevSecOps methodology assists developers and security professionals in striking a healthy balance. The use of an Agile framework allows development and security teams to collaborate continuously.

DevOps and DevSecOps methodologies are similar in many ways, including the use of automation and continuous processes to establish collaborative development cycles. While DevOps promotes delivery speed, DevSecOps promotes security.

DevSecOps practices may initially increase development time, but they will ensure that the code base is secure from the start. After some practice, and once security has been fully integrated into the development process, teams will benefit from increased writing and delivery speed for secure code bases.

Understanding processes involved in DevSecOps

Many of the processes involved in DevSecOps are not new. Your organization will hopefully be practicing them already. The main difference will be that current processes may not be optimal for use in a DevSecOps environment.

A good starting point to look at what needs to be changed in your processes is to look at the *DevSecOps manifesto* (`https://www.devsecops.org`). In a similar way to the Agile manifesto, the DevSecOps manifesto lays out nine points to mature your information security practice. These are as follows:

- Leaning in over and always saying no
- Data and security science over fear, uncertainty, and doubt
- Open contribution and collaboration over security-only requirements
- Consumable security services with APIs over mandated security controls
- Business-driven security scores over rubber stamp security
- Red and blue team exploit testing over relying on scans and theoretical vulnerabilities
- 24x7 proactive monitoring over reacting
- Shared threat intelligence over keeping information to ourselves
- Compliance operations over clipboards and checklists

You can see that most of what the manifesto lays out involves the maturity of your existing investments in information security and goes a long way to retracting some of the negative connotations that have become attached to information security over the years.

DevSecOps is hard, but when done well, you can significantly improve your security posture, as well as your understanding of security within your organization. To shift to the DevSecOps way of thinking, these five steps should be followed:

1. DevSecOps is a cultural change.
2. Align practices with the development workflow.
3. Demonstrable evidence that security keeps pace with velocity.
4. Change from prevention to detection.
5. Use the security budget to support the development workflow.

Let's have a look at the further five steps to understand the implementation.

DevSecOps is a cultural change

Adopting a DevSecOps approach will be a massive undertaking for most businesses, so be mindful of how significant a cultural shift it is. Start a conversation, be brave, and be the one to take the first step toward change. It will be easier to find common ground and reach an agreement if you engage in a clear and simple manner that highlights the business, efficiency, and security benefits for each organization.

Align practices with the development workflow

It is critical that when you engage in discussions with development teams, you do not bring your current security practices to the table and expect them to change the way they develop code.

Obviously, you should not disregard your security needs in terms of monitoring, risk assessment, and so on, but you must be willing to change your security practices to align with the development workflow. If you tried to base your DevSecOps approach on how you traditionally approach security, the entire speed and cadence of your production releases would stall.

Demonstrable evidence that security keeps pace with velocity

Your development, operations, or DevOps teams will most likely be hesitant to welcome your security teams or professionals into their *way of doing things*. You can overcome this hesitance by offering visibility and monitoring services, as well as collaborating to map your processes and identify opportunities to support agility.

Early on, you should be less concerned with enforcement, blocking activities, and slowing down the pipeline, and more concerned with demonstrating that security can keep up with the velocity with which your development teams are building so much product to ensure that the pipeline runs smoothly.

Change from prevention to detection

Once security has established itself in the development workflow, you can consider shifting from a monitoring and visibility role to proactively identifying vulnerabilities in code. The security team can become the development team's best friend in this situation.

Using your security budget to support the development workflow

Finally, consider your own security budget. Are there any areas where you can redirect some security budget to that workflow pipeline as you change your practices to align with the development workflow? This demonstrates your commitment to the sustainability of security in every release by devoting additional resources to the continuous integration and continuous deployment pipeline.

Understanding tools involved in DevSecOps

As DevSecOps is closely aligned from a process perspective with the DevOps life cycle, the tooling involved in DevSecOps closely aligns with the flow of the DevOps life cycle. The tooling in DevSecOps therefore lines up with the eight different phases of DevOps. These are the phases, along with common security tooling and processes, that you might find at each point:

- **Plan**: Threat modeling
- **Code**: Static analysis and code review
- **Build**: Penetration testing
- **Test**: Compliance validation
- **Release**: Logging
- **Deploy**: Auditing
- **Operate**: Threat intelligence
- **Monitor**: Detect, respond, recover

Next, let's have a look at some of these in more detail to understand some specifics regarding the tooling used.

Threat modeling

Unfortunately, threat modeling has long been regarded as a time-consuming and labor-intensive activity. As a result, as organizations adopt a DevSecOps approach, threat modeling is frequently left out of the security practices employed. However, the importance of thread modeling in development should not be underestimated.

According to the *2020 DevSecOps Insights Report* (`https://snyk.io/wp-content/uploads/dso_2020.pdf`), threat modeling has a significant positive impact on a team's overall confidence in their code's security.

At its core, threat modeling is intended to examine planned software to identify what might go wrong if an attacker targets that software. The purpose of this analysis is to inform the development team about which security controls should be considered as part of their implementation. Traditionally, threat modeling has been done with a broad scope across the entire application context. As part of this process, data flow diagrams, detailed threat analysis frameworks, and prescriptive threat prioritization methodologies are frequently used.

Static analysis

Static analysis tools, or **Static Application Security Testing (SAST)**, work well with almost any software automation toolchain, as well as any development methodology and process. This is primarily because they can be used locally by developers at their desktop for instantaneous feedback and to analyze a complete build, whether it is done hourly or at whatever other cadence.

Furthermore, because they do not require interaction with testers or developers, SAST tools are completely autonomous. They are useful whenever it is necessary to check the code for bugs and security vulnerabilities.

Although not a panacea when used alone, these tools should be used in tandem with other automation tools. As software teams begin to integrate security into their DevOps processes, tools such as *SonarQube* (`https://www.sonarqube.org`) are simple to implement and integrate into the automation pipeline. By detecting vulnerabilities early and preventing them from entering later in the development cycle, the pipeline pays off in reducing security fixes later.

Penetration testing

While automated tools in your pipeline can go a long way to detecting many different vulnerabilities, you will likely still have a need for penetration testing tools. Traditionally speaking, penetration testing is an art and a science in many ways. You would be forgiven for thinking that penetration testing and the focus on speed, frequency, and repeatability with DevOps would mean DevOps and penetration testing are juxtaposed.

BreachLock (`https://www.breachlock.com`), for example, can be fully integrated into a DevOps environment by performing end-to-end security testing for your product, ensuring the speed, reliability, and consistency of your development process.

Threat intelligence

Visibility for threat intelligence grows as more components of the environment are defined and documented in code. Many organizations struggle to identify their IT assets in such a way that threat intelligence can be effectively linked to the assets in their environment. By ensuring that processes are in place to feed metadata from the DevSecOps pipeline to threat intelligence capabilities, the organization can ensure that the right intelligence is gathered and applied, and responded to in a risk-prioritized manner.

We now have an understanding of what DevSecOps is, what it tries to achieve when implemented correctly, as well as an understanding of the processes and tooling involved in the DevSecOps life cycle. Now, let's look at the GitOps ecosystem.

Understanding the GitOps ecosystem

GitOps is a technique for implementing continuous deployment in cloud-native applications. It focuses on providing a developer-centric experience when operating infrastructure by utilizing tools that developers are already familiar with, such as Git and continuous deployment tools.

The core concept of GitOps is to have a Git repository that always contains declarative descriptions of the infrastructure that is currently desired in the production environment, as well as an automated process to match the described state in the repository. If you want to deploy a new application or update an existing one, all you have to do is update the repository; the automated process will handle the rest. It's like having cruise control for managing your production applications.

> **Tip**
> While we are specifically talking about Git, you can use any source control repository to achieve the same results.

GitOps provides a complete history of how your environment has changed over time. This makes error recovery as simple as running `git revert` and watching your environment restore itself.

GitOps enables you to manage deployments entirely from within your environment. Your environment only requires access to your repository and image registry for this purpose. That is all there is to it. You are not required to grant your developers direct access to the environment.

When you use Git to store complete descriptions of your deployed infrastructure, everyone on your team can see how it evolves over time. With excellent commit messages, anyone can easily reproduce the thought process of changing infrastructure and find examples of how to set up new systems.

The deployment process in GitOps is organized around code repositories as the central element. There are at least two repositories, one for the application and one for the environment configuration. The application repository contains the application's source code as well as the deployment manifests used to deploy the application.

The environment configuration repository contains all deployment manifests for a deployment environment's currently desired infrastructure. It specifies which applications and infrastructure services should be run in the deployment environment and with what configuration and version.

GitOps is a highly effective workflow pattern for managing modern cloud infrastructure. Despite its primary focus on Kubernetes cluster management, the DevOps community is applying and publishing GitOps solutions to non-Kubernetes systems. GitOps can benefit an engineering team in a variety of ways, including improved communication, visibility, stability, and system reliability.

Understanding processes involved in GitOps

The great thing about GitOps is that you don't need to be doing anything differently. If you are already writing infrastructure as code and you store your code in a repository, then you are almost there already.

The hardest thing is moving from an imperative method of deployment to a declarative method of deployment. Infrastructure as code promotes a declarative approach to system administration, which has led to the development of tools such as Ansible, Terraform, and Kubernetes, which all use static files to declare configuration.

Consider the following imperative statements, which are steps for deploying an application:

1. Install the operating system.

2. Install these dependencies.

3. Download the application from this URL.

4. Move the application to this directory.

5. Repeat this thrice on three other servers.

The declarative version of this would simply be something like *Four machines have an application from this URL, installed at this directory*. Instead of a sequence of commands, declarative software follows a declaration of an expected state.

A pipeline platform is required to complete a full GitOps installation. Some popular pipeline tools that complement GitOps include Jenkins, Azure DevOps pipelines, and CircleCI. Pipelines automate and connect Git pull requests to the orchestration system. Commands are sent to the orchestration piece after pipeline hooks are established and triggered by pull requests.

The processes involved in GitOps are therefore not really that much different from the same phases involved in the software development life cycle. Those processes define how code should be stored, what language should be used, who should review, how pipelines should be built, and where those pipelines are executed.

To achieve GitOps, you can extend what you already do in DevOps for software engineering and apply it to the infrastructure world.

Understanding tools involved in GitOps

As we touched on in the previous section, two tools are required to get started with GitOps. These tools are version control in the form of Git, as well as a tool to build and execute pipelines.

Git is the design center in the GitOps pipeline model. It serves as the source of authority for everything in the system, from code to configuration, and the entire stack. Building deployable artifacts necessitates the use of continuous integration, build, and test services. However, in the GitOps pipeline, the overall delivery orchestration is coordinated by the deployment and release automation system, which is triggered by repository updates. To summarize, continuous deployment, not continuous integration, owns delivery orchestration. It is a very subtle shift in how pipelines work from the software development life cycle. Any continuous integration provider should be able to adopt this model.

Summary

In this chapter, we have looked at XOps in detail as well as at the various operating models that are available. We have looked at DevSecOps, DataOps, and GitOps in further detail to understand their origins, benefits, processes, and tooling, looking at how this differs from DevOps.

In the next chapter, we look to bring together everything we have learned so far, review some key learnings, and walk through an example implementation of DevOps using an example organization, listing their challenges, what can be done to resolve these challenges, and finally how to implement those changes.

Questions

Let's now recap some of what we have learned throughout this chapter:

1. What does FinOps set out to achieve?

   a) Manage financial operations in cloud platforms.

   b) Set appropriate budgets.

   c) Ensure accountability for consumption.

   d) Increase agility.

2. What differentiates DevOps and DataOps?

   a) DataOps focuses on data and not software.

   b) DataOps focuses on database management.

   c) DataOps is not an iterative process like DevOps.

   d) No difference; both are the same.

12

Implementing DevOps in a Real-World Organization

Using everything we have learned so far, in this chapter we will look at putting everything into practice and see how you might implement DevOps in a real-world organization. Using a fictitious organization, we will set out problem statements, define what their goals are, and then look at how we can help that company adapt and change, starting on the road to DevOps transformation.

By the end of this chapter, you will have learned how to combine all the elements we have covered in the book and put them together to practice a real-world transformation to DevOps.

In this chapter, we're going to cover the following topics:

- Understanding why organizations move to DevOps
- Defining our fictional organization
- Walk-through of a sample DevOps transformation

Understanding why organizations move to DevOps

In *Chapter 1, Introducing DevOps and Agile*, we discussed the goals of DevOps, as well as some of the values of DevOps and the challenges that DevOps will help us solve. What about why organizations move to DevOps? This is a question we will now look at in more detail.

According to the *2019 DORA State of DevOps Report* (`https://cloud.google.com/devops/state-of-devops`), top performers in DevOps deliver code faster, have fewer bugs, and resolve incidents more quickly. Some of the highlights from that report include the following statistics backing up the previous statement:

- 208 times more frequent code deployments

- 106 times faster lead time from commit to deploy

- 2,604 times faster time to recover from incidents

- 7 times lower change failure rate

Organizations that embrace DevOps practices simply get more done. By utilizing a single team comprising cross-functional members all working in collaboration, DevOps organizations can deliver with maximum speed, functionality, and innovation.

In *Chapter 2, Business Benefits, Team Topologies, and Pitfalls of DevOps*, we focused on looking at the key business benefits of DevOps. However, you can put the benefits associated with DevOps into three clear buckets:

- Business benefits

- Technical benefits

- Cultural benefits

When we talked about business benefits, we covered things that make a business tick; things such as a boost in productivity, better-quality products, and improved employee retention were three of these reasons. Also, there are things that directly contribute to the success of the business, such as improved growth, customer satisfaction, and customer experience.

Let's now look at some of the technical and cultural benefits your organization can expect to achieve from implementing DevOps.

Technical benefits

You could list numerous technical benefits associated with DevOps. However, when you are working toward DevOps transformation, it is important to not focus on the minute details too much and to try and keep your eye on the broader benefits. The reason for this is that often those smaller benefits, while beneficial to you or your team, may not be broader benefits for other teams, the department, or your organization.

Keeping that organizational view will ensure you get maximum buy-in. Teams across the organization will feel similar benefits specific to their team, and that is great, but you must focus on the bigger benefits.

Three benefits stand out for me as critical and align with the preceding scenario of thinking about the bigger picture. They are continuous software delivery, faster resolution of problems, and less complexity. This also presents the opportunity to provide more proactive and reactive management of technical debt.

Continuous integration and continuous deployment and delivery are cornerstones of DevOps and are clear technical benefits. When implemented correctly, not only do they provide you clear benefits around the building and deployment of your applications but they provide a means to catch bad practices during development, as well as catching security issues and threats along the way.

With the practices employed in DevOps, you are making your environment less complex. This reduction in complexity is attractive to organizations as well as individual teams. The best thing is that the reduction in complexity can be in a number of areas, such as your workflows, meaning you've automated manual tasks; it could be in the production of documentation, for example. It also means removing unnecessary steps from your processes. This comes in the form of value stream mapping exercises to identify and remove them from your operation.

Finally, with the improvement in the monitoring of your application and infrastructure that comes with DevOps also comes site reliability engineering, which is to do with the ability to recover from failures quickly. **Site reliability engineering (SRE)** is a discipline that applies aspects of software engineering to infrastructure and operations problems.

The level of telemetry provided and the shared understanding between teams on the application and infrastructure supports the application as well as the goals set out by the teams.

Cultural benefits

Throughout the chapters, we have talked heavily about the influence of culture in DevOps. Culture in DevOps is what binds our teams together. Happier, more productive teams; greater professional development opportunities; and higher employee engagement are three of the big cultural benefits you can achieve from a successful implementation of DevOps.

I just talked about the shared responsibilities in teams that come with DevOps. This is a big driver for cultural benefits. When teams are invested in shared responsibilities, common goals, and driving vision, this creates a culturally sound working environment that drives happier teams that are more productive.

One further benefit to this is the higher employee engagement from the good culture that DevOps can breed. We are taught in DevOps the notions "fail fast" and "growth mindset." Both of these mean employees are more likely to voice their ideas and be open with each other because the focus is not on blame; the focus is on making things better and sharing ideas to achieve the common goal.

Finally, when you put all of these things together, you broaden the skills of your team quite naturally. You provide people with the tools and the capabilities to expand their knowledge and further their careers. Organizations with true career growth opportunities are one of the biggest things new hires will look for. DevOps can help your organization be attractive for new hires.

Balancing stability against new features

In a non-DevOps environment, there is often a conflict between releasing new features and maintaining stability. The development team is evaluated based on the number of updates delivered to users, whereas the operations team is evaluated based on the overall health of the system.

In a DevOps environment, everyone on the team is responsible for delivering new features as well as stability. Because code isn't *thrown over the wall* to operations at the end of development, the combination of a shared code base, continuous integration, test-driven techniques, and automated deployments, among other things, exposes issues in application code, infrastructure, or configuration earlier in the process.

Because change sets are smaller, problems tend to be less complex. DevOps engineers can use real-time data on system performance to quickly understand the impact of application changes. And resolution times are reduced because team members do not have to wait for a different team to troubleshoot and resolve the issue.

Increased effectiveness

In a typical IT environment, there is enormous waste as people wait for other people and other machines—or they are stuck solving the same problems over and over. Employees prefer to be productive, and time spent churning causes frustration and unhappiness. Everyone benefits when people can spend less time on unsatisfying aspects of their jobs and more time on adding value to the organization.

Key aspects of DevOps models of IT operations are automated deployments and standardized production environments, which make deployments predictable and free people from routine repetitive tasks to do more high-value things. For example, a large financial services firm with over 4,000 IT employees saved over $8 million by implementing DevOps, which reduced MTTR and eliminated legacy tool maintenance.

Now we have looked more broadly at the reasons organizations move to DevOps. Let's now define our fictional organization to look at the implementation of a DevOps transformation.

Defining our fictional organization

Before we look at our transformation journey, let's first define the organization we are working with. I would like to introduce you all to *Travelics*. Through early discussions with Travelics, we have found out some usual details from them:

- Global organization based in Europe and North America.

- Employs around 4,000 employees.

- Produces two products for the aviation industry, one focused on baggage tracking and one on operational insights.

- Both products have teams of around 15 developers.

- Operations is a shared entity and part of central IT.

Now that we have established some fundamentals about Travelics, let's move into learning some more specifics about them and what they are trying to achieve.

Current operating model

Travelics' current operating model is that customers drive feature requests to the software engineering teams. The process of doing this is via engagement with account managers as well as industry experience from engineers on the team. All requests are centrally managed and distributed to teams responsible for that feature. The work is undertaken and queued for release.

The operations team is a shared entity that is part of the central IT team. They rely on documentation from the development team to troubleshoot the application. The application is currently undergoing a transformation from being a monolithic application that is deployed on virtual machines in a public cloud environment to being one that is more cloud-native and relies on microservices and multi-tenanted software as a service model.

Currently, virtual machines are deployed for each new client and if the client buys both software packages, these will sit on separate instances.

Challenges that exist within the current model

The current ways of working provide a number of challenges for Travelics. The biggest is that they are not agile enough in how they deliver their applications. Releases only happen twice a year; this often results in failures at deployment and rollback of the application while the issues are resolved. This outage can often be around four hours.

Another issue is the quality of code: developers are highly skilled but there is a general lack of review and oversight of each other's work. This leads to bugs, and the engineering teams have a large list of technical debt that needs addressing.

The lack of scalability and cloud-native approach is also limiting. This provides serious operational challenges and results in different configuration approaches for different customers; versions of the application are not consistent across all customers and some customers also have unsupported versions deployed as they are unwilling to allow the company to upgrade them over the fear of outages.

Understanding of DevOps varies throughout the engineering organization, and outside of engineering, not many employees may understand DevOps. Pockets of people understand what DevOps is, but there is general hesitancy to move toward a different model.

Goals for the future

A driving factor for change is the introduction of a new organization providing similar services. This disruptor is much smaller but is able to deliver new features quickly and runs a completely "software as a service" solution. Travelics has lost three large customers already to this competitor. They believe that with changes, they can address these problems and compete once again.

Travelics has the following goals for their DevOps transformation:

- Clear vision for the development of the products
- Agility that allows teams to work independently but share practices

- Focus on faster releases and increased quality

- Increase customer satisfaction

- Realize new features more quickly

- Reduce the amount of failures

- Move to a more modern platform capable of scaling

In summary, our DevOps transformation for Travelics needs to look at the organization from top to bottom. This includes how the teams are structured as well as how they operate. These changes will be fundamental to how Travelics works and, if successful, will make a big difference to the way they operate.

Let's now begin the DevOps transformation journey for Travelics.

Walk-through of DevOps transformation

Now we understand the outline of the Travelics organization, as well as their current situation and aspirations and goals for the future. We can start engaging with them on making their goals a reality.

A number of steps exist for a successful transformation; it's a long process. The complexities involved in transforming large enterprises necessitate buy-in at the highest level to make this successful and implement the changes that are required. The steps you would look to take for a transformation would be as follows:

1. Have initial planning workshops.

2. Establish a DevOps Center of Excellence.

3. Set up governance of the transformation.

4. Establish an intake process.

5. Identify and initiate pilots.

6. Assess current capabilities.

7. Perform transformation exercises.

8. Scale out the DevOps transformation.

Now, let's look at these steps in more detail and discuss the specifics we need to do with Travelics to achieve their goals.

Having initial planning workshops

Participants must include all of the towers that comprise the solution delivery. Along with operations, security, and development, business participation is required. I always recommend that the workshops in this step be led by an experienced external consultant or coach. The key here is to gain executive support and to establish common goals and understanding of what a DevOps program will entail:

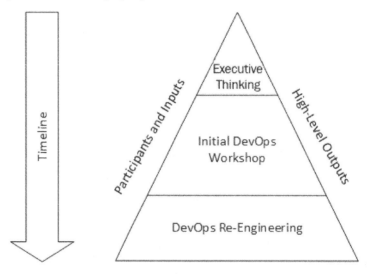

Figure 12.1 – Diagram showing the inputs and outputs of your initial planning

For Travelics, the initial planning is really important. Remember we said that other than a few pockets of people, many people do not understand DevOps, and with this comes some hesitancy to move to a new way of working.

Typically, several small DevOps programs exist in silos and lack the maturity to scale to the enterprise level. Design thinking is an excellent method to employ because it capitalizes on the expertise of all stakeholders, enables them to reach a common understanding, and establishes the necessary buy-in.

Now we will look at the elements needed to build a DevOps center of excellence, which is a critical step in the adoption of DevOps.

Establishing a DevOps Center of Excellence

Creating a **Center of Excellence (CoE)** is inadequate if it is not at the appropriate organizational level and enterprise authority. It must be led by a business leader who has the support and buy-in of all towers. Representatives from all delivery towers, as well as vendor organizations, are active participants in the CoE. These participants must be chosen with caution.

Building on the diagram in *Figure 12.1*, we can now add several other elements to it as we define the stakeholders needed and more tightly define the outputs.

You should note the timeline is pointing down in the diagram; this means starting your conversations at the top. For the transformational challenges faced by Travelics, my recommendation would be having either the CEO or COO be responsible from a sponsorship perspective in the transformation.

> **Tip**
> Although the timeline is top down, there is nothing wrong with gaining sponsorship from the bottom up as well. This is just a formal way of establishing a formal CoE.

Starting from day one of the transformation, executives from the software engineering teams and senior leaders from operations, development, and even the CTO or CIO should be involved in those early discussions.

The output of this stage is to establish a common mindset for the DevOps transformation. This will be establishing common goals, objectives, and priorities for the work that needs to be done.

Around three to five days into the process, our discussion needs to evolve to a further level of detail and include the program owner, who is also a sponsor of the project. This needs to include representatives from the following areas:

- Application owners
- Enterprise architecture
- Solution architects
- Development leads
- Operations leads

Over the next two weeks, workshops take place with Travelics to perform value stream mapping of the software development life cycle. The goal of this is to further understand in detail the current state of the organization, development state, detailed delivery processes, and any key performance indicators currently attributed to performance.

These workshops at this stage also look to expand out of areas that are to be prioritized from an impact perspective. Given the needs described about Travelics, which do you think is a priority area for them?

> **Tip**
> Travelics are losing customers and experiencing issues due to quality. This dictates that an immediate area for improvement is customer satisfaction and the quality of releases.

Finally, somewhere around 20 days into the initial planning process, the same group of people as before come back around the table to look at a deep dive into how engineering will look at the end of the process.

Taking into account everything that we know about Travelics and their high-level goals and ambitions, this should drive these workshops forward and help provide the detail needed to form a plan and direction of travel.

The expected outputs from these final planning workshops would expect to produce future state mapping and reference architecture for DevOps. At this point, we should have at least a draft of an implementation roadmap with high-level targets introduced.

One thing that is clear at this stage is that the current team structure is not fit for purpose and does not align with the goals of Travelics. Therefore, outputs also include the proposed structure for the teams going forward as well as defining any roles and responsibilities.

The final part of this section includes creating a business case for moving forward with the transformation and an executive summary of what the proposal contains.

I strongly advise that the initial phases of the CoE be led by an external experienced partner and then transitioned over time. The initial phases aid in the consolidation of the CoE's vision and strategies, as well as the establishment of best practices to support them. Typically, it takes 12 to 24 months to transition from business partner to internal stakeholders.

Setting up governance of the transformation

This is the most important step in changing the organization's culture. The roles and responsibilities of practitioners will change as a result of Agile and DevOps. To succeed, they will require awareness, enablement, and empowerment. It is critical that they understand the collaboration between organizations that have historically had animosity between them in order to break down these organizational walls. KPIs must shift away from individual metrics and toward overall customer business outcomes.

Establishing governance is not as hard as it is made to sound. Your program governance consists of three main things: communication plans, an enablement program, and established KPIs.

Your communication plan involves frequently publicizing your program objectives, milestones, and successes. From an enablement perspective, this needs to be looking at Agile fundamentals for your business leaders, so they understand the critical elements. Enablement also includes starting to look at platform and toolchain education for those teams as well as deeper training on DevOps approaches such as continuous integration, continuous deployment, continuous testing, and continuous feedback and improvement.

Finally, your KPIs must come from solid key metrics, a good strategy to measure, and a frequent and detailed reporting cadence as well as milestones for the transformation.

Establishing an intake process

The first sprint that onboards the program sets the tone for the rest of the sprints. It is not so much a matter of tools and processes as it is of the proper sizing of tools and processes. The selection of accelerators, tool chains, and development methods must be fit for purpose. Once established, the intake process must be communicated throughout the organization. Collect feedback and evolve and mature on a continuous basis.

Reusable assets are key to having an effective intake process. Architectural patterns, automation scripts, operational cookbooks, and infrastructure assets are all critical assets that can be defined and agreed once and reused in multiple different scenarios.

The success of sprints comes down to best practices. These best practices help enforce consistency and help provide repeatable results across not only pilot teams but also for when the transformation is scaled up. Ensuring you have defined practices for trunk-based development patterns, branching and merging strategies for your source control, and test automation patterns and processes around test-driven development as well as continuous integration are keys to success at this stage.

Identifying and initiating pilots

When applied to a specific portfolio of applications or a domain solution, this step has the best chance of success. Prior to this workshop, I strongly advise opening some working sessions to identify an area of development work that represents a portfolio to scale to the enterprise.

The goal of this step is to conduct a value stream mapping exercise with participants from all towers for a specific application. This must be done in sufficient detail to identify the current end-to-end process, tooling, manual and automated processes, as well as the skills and people involved.

The collaboration of **subject matter experts** (**SMEs**) from the CoE with the project team is the next step in the project intake process. The goal is to provide advice on the "to-be" process, including the necessary tooling, reusable assets, automation, and SMEs from operations, security, and other relevant areas. The application Scrum team will be made up of these SMEs. Identified KPIs for the program are captured as the application goes through its development/test cycle. This is absolutely required for comparison with existing KPIs.

Assessment of current capabilities

Understanding the pockets of DevOps that exist in your organization is really important. Some of those pockets may be more mature than you realize, and you may be able to take some of the good practices already in place and use them in other parts of your transformation.

These assessments can be done in a number of ways, but it needs to be something that is repeatable, as you will need to reuse these assessments throughout your transformation in order to check your progress and realign if needed. Assessments need to be broad and detailed.

Over time, the ambition should be to run assessments with the team, have them score each question using a set of cards, and discuss the scores among the team to agree on actions for improvement.

One of the best assessments I have found is one from Marc Hornbeek who is the founder of *Engineering DevOps* (https://img1.wsimg.com/blobby/go/1c453e6b-8ce5-4e3d-a110-bba77def37c3/downloads/DevOps%20Practices%20Maturity%20Assessment%20v2.xlsx?ver=1619731527627). This assessment is comprehensive and free to use. It covers in detail the nine pillars of a DevOps practice, which include the following:

- Collaborative culture practices
- Continuous security practices

- Continuous monitoring practices

- Design for DevOps practices

- Continuous delivery practices

- Elastic infrastructure practices

- Continuous testing practices

- Continuous integration practices

- Collaborative leadership practices

These comprehensive questions give a rounded view of performance. Using the same assessment provides you with a clear view of improvement in performance over time and something you can look back on to track over time:

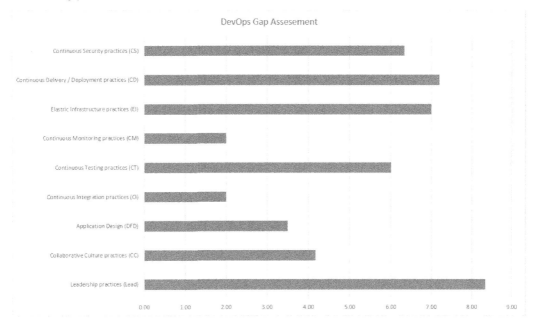

Figure 12.2 – Example output from a maturity assessment

As you can see from the preceding diagram, the output provides us with a comprehensive snapshot. Each question has the ability to set the importance of that question to your organization and assess your current score. The top bar in the group indicates your maturity score in this area:

DevOps Practices GAP Summary	(I) Importance	(P) Practice Level	(G) GAP	RANK	# Practices	Comments
Leadership practices (Lead)	5.0	3.2	8.3	1	5	
Collaborative Culture practices (CC)	2.7	2.7	4.2	6	7	
Design For DevOps (DFD)	3.5	3.3	3.5	7	9	
Continuous Integration practices (CI)	3.8	3.3	2.0	8	6	
Continuous Testing practices (CT)	3.1	4.1	6.0	5	9	
Continuous Monitoring practices (CM)	1.5	2.8	2.0	8	7	
Elastric Infrastructure practices (EI)	2.9	3.0	7.0	3	9	
Continuous Delivery / Deployment practices	3.2	2.7	7.2	2	7	
Continuous Security practices (CS)	3.3	3.0	6.3	4	8	
Overall Assessment (Average)	3.2	3.1	5.2		67	
	Importance	Practice Level	GAP		Total	

Figure 12.3 – Example detailed output from maturity assessment

The output also provides a per pillar view of your maturity. This gives you an idea of the priority areas by calculating the level of importance against the current score, meaning the lowest score becomes the highest area for improvement.

Periodically, we should also look at performing more detailed assessments as well. This change-up asks different questions and challenges in certain other focus areas. The more detailed assessment looks at the following areas:

- DevOps training practices
- DevOps governance practices
- DevOps value stream management practices
- DevOps application performance monitoring practices
- DevOps SRE practices
- DevOps service catalog practices
- DevOps application release automation practices
- DevOps multi-cloud practices

- DevOps Infrastructure as Code practices

- DevOps hybrid cloud practices

- DevOps version management practices

This highly detailed assessment takes a while to run. When running this with teams previously, I would set aside a morning to complete the discussions and include time for breaks to keep people fresh.

In a similar way to the nine-pillar output, the output from the detailed assessment is the same in providing a sample chart documenting maturity and a table overview looking at highlighting areas of priority focus:

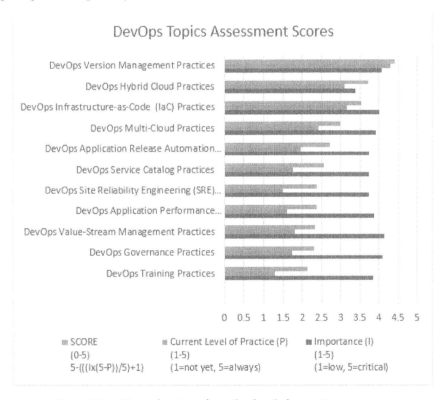

Figure 12.4 – Example output from the detailed maturity assessment

Other assessments for specific roles are also available at the *Engineering DevOps* (https://engineeringdevops.com/documents#bf990569-1a3f-4eb4-bb3b-73073abf8a31) website. These are incredibly useful resources to assist with your transformation and improvement journeys.

Performing transformation exercises

Performing the action tasks that need to be executed to move the transformation forward obviously depends on the output of the planning workshops. Looking back at our example of Travelics, let's now look at some tasks we would do to aid with their DevOps transformation.

- The Chocolate, LEGO, and Scrum game
- Introduction to Agile
- Transforming to Agile working
- Reorganizing the team structure
- Looking at process improvement
- Implementing DevOps practices
- Getting on the feedback loop

Let's now look at these areas specifically to look at how we would help Travelics achieve their goals.

Chocolate, LEGO, and Scrum game

The initial workshops provide an opportunity to level set on DevOps with a wider audience and to gain trust with the people you are working with. Consider using a simulation workshop rather than running through slides to promote the benefits of DevOps.

In order to do this, I would consider the *Chocolate, LEGO, and Scrum* game by Dana Pylayeva (`https://www.slideshare.net/danapylayeva/introduction-to-devops-with-lego-and-choco`). The simulation game provides participants with the opportunity to hear the same real-world struggles they face and then act out scenarios that remove these blockers so they can see the results of removing them.

This is a powerful exercise that, in my experience, is more powerful than a simple slide deck explaining the benefits of DevOps. The aim of the game is for people to sit in groups, then using a set of role cards that determine the specific activities, people can run through time-boxed exercises we call sprints.

The aim is to sell LEGO animals on the marketplace and produce as many as you can that meet the requirements stated. As each sprint begins, roles change and blockers are removed, improving the chances of delivering more.

Introduction to Agile

In this session, aimed at operations teams within Travelics, we are directly appealing to people who are generally more swayed against Agile. Development teams, in my experience, are more likely to be comfortable with Agile working. The principles are born out of software engineering; that does not mean that you cannot work with operations teams, though.

It is a common misconception that operations teams cannot operate in an Agile manner. In my opinion and experience, this is simply not true. I will shortly explain why and how we can address some of the common concerns of operations teams who are working to Agile methods. We start by asking three simple questions (and each attendee has a stack of sticky notes):

- Why is it worth doing?

- How is it difficult?

- What is Agile?

Each attendee is then given around five minutes to write down answers and put them under the appropriate heading. Then we head to a discussion with the team, talk about the notes they have written down, and try and get an open conversation going. When appropriate, anyone running the workshop can then use experience in this field to provide examples to back up or counter the discussion.

If possible, invite someone from a team that is already on an Agile transformation or already practices some of the qualities we are trying to highlight. Look to invite someone this team trusts; they will value their opinion more than yours at this stage. Luckily, we have someone at Travelics who matches this profile. They had difficulty closing work down after development and an element of their work was ticket-based. For this reason, our CoE asked for someone from the other team to come in and join the discussion.

This worked well for several reasons, mainly because the team we were delivering the workshop to had someone from another team who was going through this transformation and could attest to the things we were saying. Mostly, this individual could attest that this process works and it's worth paying more than just lip service to.

Transformation to Agile working

The plan to transform the team comes in three steps. Individually, the steps are small, but together they form the journey:

1. Introduce daily standups.

2. Introduce work management such as stories and introduce Scrumban.

3. Introduce planning, sprints, and retrospectives.

During the initial workshop with Travelics, we held the team's first ever standup. The concept of the daily standup is aimed at answering three things:

- What did I work on yesterday?

- What am I working on today?

- What issues are blocking me?

In sport, a huddle is strategic, keeping everyone informed and connected throughout the game. For technology teams, the standup is a huddle; it's designed to enforce the *we* and *one team* culture and mentality.

Highlighting issues to the team often results in someone else in the team helping unblock them. Your standup should be no longer than 15 minutes. Don't go into the minute details of your day. Keep it at a high level and keep it relevant. Highlight issues, but don't discuss them in detail.

The next day, someone from the CoE team attended the second daily standup this team ran. They only started the day before and it took around five minutes to complete. Everyone kept it simple, highlighting what they worked on and what they were working on. Blockers were discussed at a high level and agreement was taken to move the conversation offline. So, from a session the week before, in less than 30 minutes of meeting time, this team were already starting to get in sync with each other more than they were before.

By now, we are already a little into this piece of work and one of the most important aspects of Agile is the introduction of retrospectives. Most teams, in fact, regardless of their Agile working status, already do some kind of retrospective, usually a team meeting. A retrospective or retro just focuses the mind on the last sprint. We ask different questions depending on the type of retro the Scrum master is running. You can get a number of different types of retros to run, such as 4 Ls, speedcar, starfish, and many others.

The 4 Ls retrospective involves asking participants to add up cards under four headings: Liked, Learned, Lacked, and Longed For. This asks the team to discuss and highlight the positives and negatives.

The speedcar retrospective, similar to the following example, is about highlighting the things that made the team move faster and things that slowed them down.

The starfish retrospective, like the 4 Ls, asks the team to focus on what the team should do less or more, or start, stop, or keep doing. The principle is to foster thinking around the value the team gets from different practices in the team. The starfish retrospective is an important one when working in continuous feedback loops.

For the first retrospective, the CoE team decided to run one of the most basic ones out there; this was the sailboat retro. In this, we draw a sailboat, add an anchor, and ask the team to place things that made the team go faster near the sail and things that dragged the team down near the anchor, as you can see in the following diagram:

Figure 12.5 – Example drawing showing the concept of a sailboat retrospective

This exercise is really simple and the feedback from the team was that they enjoyed the daily standups; they also enjoyed finding out more about what others in the team were up to and the Kanban style of working for visually highlighting where work is.

Things that did not work for the team were the additional meeting time, as well as a feeling that sometimes the standups went on for too long and that the value was maybe not as high as they expected.

> **Important note**
>
> While we are quite statistics-heavy in Agile, you can progress well and teach people the required skills and ways of working and see improvements without the need for a heavy focus on statistics. Improvements in metrics will come in time.

It sounds crude, but propaganda is important when you are fundamentally changing how organizations work. Consider placing posters around the office environment and posting them out on communications channels. You can use the free posters from *Dandy People* (`https://dandypeople.com/posters`) as tools to aid in the messaging.

Reorganizing the team structure

Through our discussions with Travelics and our understanding of their goals, it's clear that their current team structure will not work. One of the fundamental changes is moving to a product-oriented view, away from a project view.

The product view enables us to bring in product management roles to help manage and prioritize feedback as well as helping us to use market intelligence to drive the team's decision-making on what is a priority over something else:

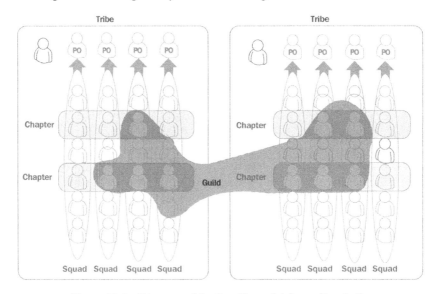

Figure 12.6 – Diagram of the Spotify model for scaling Agile

Next is the desire to bring people closer together through collaboration and have the ability to scale these teams. One suitable approach to this challenge at Travelics could be the use of the *Spotify model* (`https://www.atlassian.com/agile/agile-at-scale/spotify`). This introduces the use of terms such as **squads**, **tribes**, **chapters**, and **guilds**.

Squads

In layman's terms, a squad is a group of developers. In many ways, a squad is similar to a Scrum team in that it is intended to feel like a small start-up. These teams will typically sit together and have all of the necessary skills and tooling to design, develop, test, and release to production. Squads will decide how they want to work, which means that some will use Scrum sprints, others will use Kanban, and still others will use a combination known as Scrumban.

Every squad has a specific goal, such as developing a specific feature of an application, managing the public website, writing the mobile application, or something else. Different squads could even be in charge of different aspects of the user experience.

Squads are also encouraged to use principles such as **minimum viable product** (**MVP**), which means releasing early and frequently. I recall a quote from the first article I read about this topic by *Arthur von Kriegenbergh* (`https://medium.com/agile-series/agile-series-how-we-work-think-it-build-it-ship-it-tweak-it-afrogleap-1afb080dedab`) that used the slogan *Think it, build it, ship it, tweak it*. Because each squad is laser-focused on one mission and one component of the product for such an extended period of time, they develop into key experts.

Tribes

Tribes are collections of squads, and these tribes are all squads that work on related parts of the product. For example, in the Spotify case, all of our squads could be in a tribe for the desktop application, desktop UI, or something else; you get the idea. Each tribe also has a tribe leader, who is responsible for ensuring that the tribe has everything the squads require. All squads within a tribe should ideally sit in the same physical location, if possible. Communal areas should also encourage levels of collaboration between squads.

Have you ever heard of *Dunbar's Number*? Tribes should be sized according to this theory in an ideal world. According to this, most people are unable to maintain social relationships with more than about 100 people. When the group size exceeds this number, restrictive rules, politics, and additional layers of management add bureaucracy and other areas of inefficiencies. As a result, tribes should be designed to have fewer than 100 members.

The loss of economies is one of the challenges associated with scalability and a high degree of autonomy. For example, a developer in one squad may be working on a problem that was solved by a developer in another squad the previous week. This is precisely what chapters and guilds are designed to address.

Chapters

Chapters, like guilds, serve as the glue that holds the company together. After all, with such high levels of autonomy and no communication between squads and tribes, your company might as well be divided into many small ones. Chapters and guilds allow you to benefit from economies of scale without giving up too much autonomy.

For this reason, a chapter is a small group of people with similar skills who work in the same general area or within the same tribe. This means that developers, testers, security professionals, and any other role can really benefit from other people with similar skills who are also working in the same tribe; this glue means that within a chapter, you have deep expertise within your domain and can share skills and draw on others who understand the domain you are working in.

Guilds

Guilds are more akin to community organizations. A guild is a group of people who want to share their knowledge, tools, code, and practices. A guild is spread across the entire organization, whereas a chapter is local to a tribe. You can have as many guilds as you want in your organization; for example, consider the following:

- Testing guild
- Cloud technology guild
- Scrum guild
- Agile coaching guild

Doesn't this all sound like a matrix-style organization to you? It does, but not in the way you are accustomed to. People with similar skills are typically grouped together into functional teams and then assigned to projects, reporting to a manager of that team, who reports to a senior leader in that area. The matrix we've created and are working in here is geared toward delivery.

Consider it in two dimensions: the horizontal dimension is for sharing knowledge, tools, and code, and the vertical dimension is for sharing code. The vertical dimension is the most important, and it is where people collaborate and organize to create great products. This describes how people are physically arranged and where they spend the majority of their time. Consider the vertical dimension to be *what* and the horizontal dimension to be *how*. The matrix structure ensures that each squad member receives guidance on both *what to build next* and *how to build it well*.

Implementing DevOps practices

Getting the right practices while being backed up by the right metrics is now the focus for Travelics. Using the things we have learned throughout this chapter, we can put in place metrics.

So much about the metrics we discussed in *Chapter 3, Measuring the Success of DevOps*, comes into focus here. Remember what we have learned about the goals of Travelics. In simple terms, they want to improve quality, increase velocity, and reduce the failure rate or increase stability.

All of the metrics we discussed fall into those three categories. Here are some metrics that we can propose to help Travelics start to measure their performance going forward as they start to implement DevOps practices:

- Lead time – Travelics have a desire to improve their time to market. This metric helps them understand the amount of time it takes to take ideas from inception on the backlog to completion. Our target for this metric is 60 days; over time, this should be reduced as maturity increases.

- Deployment failure rate – Remember the complaints from customers about out-of-date software and new releases causing downtime? Well, this metric will help directly track that issue and in time, focused effort on pipelines, quality of code, and more incremental releases can help. Our target for this metric is 1%.

- Unit test coverage – Improving testing is a good way to improve quality, and introducing quality gates in releases around test coverage and test passes is key to increasing quality. Our target for this metric is 95%.

- Defect aging – Travelics also have a problem with high amounts of technical debt. Putting a metric around the age of defects is really key to getting that number down, as well as introducing technical sprints to address that technical debt. Our target for this metrics is 7 days.

- **Mean time to recovery (MTTR)** – To address the issue with outages, measuring the MTTR will place specific emphasis on the recovery time and improving that. It helps also drive levels of automated recovery within the teams and helps focus on missing elements that contribute to further downtime.

- Incidents per deployment – The last metric that will help Travelics is one that looks at the number of support incidents generated per deployment. This helps to track the satisfaction of customers in line with the release strategy as well as helping to determine further improvements that can be made.

This is also the phase at which you introduce tooling to help determine the direction of travel for process automation. When you have a baseline of metrics, introducing tooling helps you further identify areas where you can improve.

Getting on the feedback loop

Finally, at this point, your established continuous improvement and feedback loops should kick into gear more rigorously and work to evolve what the transformation team have created, putting the organization on the way to wider success.

During a transformation process, you learn a large amount about the organization, the processes it uses, and the people within it. All of these learnings are critical to feedback on the continued investment in DevOps and the continued success of Travelics.

Scaling out the DevOps transformation

The penultimate step is to take feedback from pilot metrics and scale them by running multiple release trains from various application portfolios. It is insufficient to simply perform daily builds and automated deployments. Continuous feedback and optimization are the final pieces of the DevOps puzzle.

Notice that I mentioned that this is the penultimate step. Actually, you should never finish; just because you have negotiated transformation does not mean you are finished. This is an opportunity to take what you have learned from your pilot groups and give feedback to sponsors, product owners, and stakeholders.

Summary

In this chapter, we have provided a summary of the key learning from the book and have looked at specific implementation guidance for a fictional travel company. This advice has helped drive Travelics in the right direction and they are now, after a period of 18 months, hitting consistent metric targets and looking to further improve what the CoE has developed within the organization.

As the chapter and indeed the book draws to a close, I would like to thank you for coming on the DevOps transformation journey with me. I hope that you have found the book informative and can take things we have learned together into your organizations to drive change.

Why subscribe?

Other Books You May Enjoy

If you enjoyed this book, you may be interested in these other books by Packt:

Mastering Docker - Fourth Edition

Russ McKendrick

ISBN: 978-1-83921-657-2

- Get to grips with essential Docker components and concepts
- Discover the best ways to build, store, and distribute container images
- Understand how Docker can fit into your development workflow
- Secure your containers and files with Docker's security features
- Explore first-party and third-party cluster tools and plugins
- Launch and manage your Kubernetes clusters in major public clouds

Learning DevOps

Mikael Krief

ISBN: 978-1-83864-273-0

- Become well versed with DevOps culture and its practices
- Use Terraform and Packer for cloud infrastructure provisioning
- Implement Ansible for infrastructure configuration
- Use basic Git commands and understand the Git flow process
- Build a DevOps pipeline with Jenkins, Azure Pipelines, and GitLab CI
- Containerize your applications with Docker and Kubernetes
- Check application quality with SonarQube and Postman
- Protect DevOps processes and applications using DevSecOps tools

Packt is searching for authors like you

If you're interested in becoming an author for Packt, please visit authors. packtpub.com and apply today. We have worked with thousands of developers and tech professionals, just like you, to help them share their insight with the global tech community. You can make a general application, apply for a specific hot topic that we are recruiting an author for, or submit your own idea.

Leave a review - let other readers know what you think

Please share your thoughts on this book with others by leaving a review on the site that you bought it from. If you purchased the book from Amazon, please leave us an honest review on this book's Amazon page. This is vital so that other potential readers can see and use your unbiased opinion to make purchasing decisions, we can understand what our customers think about our products, and our authors can see your feedback on the title that they have worked with Packt to create. It will only take a few minutes of your time, but is valuable to other potential customers, our authors, and Packt. Thank you!

Index

A

acceptance tests 10
ADKAR model
  about 129
  reference link 129
ADKAR model, phases
  Current 130
  Future 130
  Transition 130
Agile
  in DevOps 12
  Kanban 17
  Kanplan 17
  scaling, with Spotify model 20, 21
  Scrum 16, 17
  with DevOps 15
Agile framework methodologies
  mixing, within organizations 18
Agile manifesto
  about 13
  culture, defining 13, 14
  principles 14
  reference link 14
Agile teams
  scaling 18, 19

B

behavior-driven development (BDD) 19
better communication, DevOps culture
  about 72
  developers, performing releases 74
  developers, working in operations 75
  operations, participating in
    sprint planning 73
  operations, working in
    development sprints 74
BreachLock
  URL 204
business change models
  about 126, 127
  ADKAR model 130
  EASIER model 130

architectural requirements
  about 176, 181
  defining 182
architecture reviews
  preparing 182
automation 42

Kotter's change management
    model 127, 128
Rogers' technology adoption
    curve 128, 129

C

Center of Excellence (CoE) 217
change
  resistance 85
Cloud Native Computing
    Foundation (CNCF) 171
CloudOps 194, 195
CNCF Cloud Native Landscape
    URL 171
collaboration, DevOps culture 75
common quality metrics, to
    measure DevOps success
  about 49, 50
  code quality 50
  code vulnerabilities 51
  defect aging 50
  defect density 50
  defect reintroduction rate 51
  standards violations 51
  unit test coverage 50
common stability metrics, to
    measure DevOps success
  about 51
  change failure rate 52
  deployment downtime 52
  incidents per deployment 52
  Mean Time to Recovery (MTTR) 52
  number of hotfixes 52
  platform availability 53
  unapproved changes 52

common velocity metrics, to
    measure DevOps success
  about 47
  change volume 48
  cycle time 48
  deployment duration 47
  deployment failure rate 49
  deployment frequency 48
  environment provisioning time 49
  lead time 48
  test automation coverage 48
communication 91
communication breakdowns
  avoiding 91, 92
continuous delivery (CD) 11
continuous deployment 11, 47
continuous feedback
  about 140
  culture, building 142
  process 147
  techniques 144, 148
continuous feedback culture, key elements
  channels and tools, providing 143
  clear communication of
      vision and goals 142
  continuous feedback, purpose 143
  feedback accountability 143
  team education 144
continuous feedback techniques
  360-degree feedback 148
  about 148
  EDGE framework 148
  feedback ratios 149
continuous improvement
  about 46, 140
  culture, building 140
  process 144
  techniques 144

continuous improvement process
  about 144
  action, taking 145
  future, planning 146
  opportunities, identifying 145
  results, studying 146
  root cause, analyzing 145
  solution, standardizing 146
  techniques 146
continuous improvement techniques
  about 146
  catchball 147
  daily huddles 146, 147
  gemba walks 147
continuous integration (CI) 10, 11
continuous integration/continuous
    delivery (CI/CD) principles 42

D

daily standup 146
DataOps
  development process 197, 198
  ecosystem 195-197
DataOps, tools
  about 198
  automation of processes
    and workflow 199
  communication and process
    management, implementing 199
  consistent deployment 199
  data, adding 199
  logic tests, adding 199
  source control management 198
defect leakage 51
DevOps
  Agile 12
  challenges, addressing 8

challenges, solving 7, 8
for process improvement 105
goals 4-6
reasons, for organizations move 210
values 6, 7
with Agile 15
DevOps Advocates 31
DevOps as a service 30
DevOps, benefits
  cultural benefits 212
  increased effectiveness 213
  stability, balancing 212
  technical benefits 211
DevOps culture
  about 66
  better communication 72, 73
  collaboration, across teams 75
  maintaining 76-79
  retrospectives 68-70
  roles and responsibilities
    workshop 66, 67
  rules of engagement 68
  significance 70
  transparency, increasing 71
DevOps ecosystem 158
DevOps, key business benefits
  about 24
  business growth 25
  cost savings 25
  customer experience (CX) 25
  employee retention, improving 26
  higher customer satisfaction 26
  operational and process efficiency,
    improving 26, 27
  productivity 25
  quality products 26

DevOps maturity, phases
  about 8
  continuous delivery (CD) 11
  continuous deployment 11
  continuous integration (CI) 10, 11
  waterfall 9, 10
DevOps tooling
  benefits 166-169
  obstacles 170-172
DevOps tools 158
DevOps tools, phases
  building 159, 160
  collaborating 158, 159
  deploying 160
  running 161
  testing 160
DevOps transformation
  about 215
  Center of Excellence (CoE),
    establishing 217, 218
  current capabilities assessment 220-223
  exercise, performing 224
  governance, setting up 219
  initial planning workshops 216
  intake process, establishing 219
  pilots, identifying 220
  pilots, initiating 220
DevOps transformation failure
  automation and speed 42
  culture, impact 41
  culture, setting 41
  decoding 41
  DevOps for organization, defining 42
  teamwork 42, 43
DevOps transformation tasks
  Agile 225
  Agile, working 226, 227
  Chocolate, LEGO, and Scrum game 224

feedback loop, establishing 232
performing 224
practices, implementing 231
scaling out 232
team structure, reorganizing 228
DevSecOps
  development process 201, 202
  ecosystem 199, 200
  URL 201
DevSecOps, tools
  about 203
  penetration testing 204
  static analysis tools 204
  threat intelligence 205
  threat modeling 203
direct impact
  about 131
  people comfort zone 132
  social arrangement disruption 132
  status lowering 132

E

EASIER model 130
effective communication
  collaboration tools 152
  group-wide emails 152
  working groups 151
enterprise architecture
  actionable deliverables, creating 178
  agility, increasing 178
  benefits 176-178
  management of complexity 177
  time to value, reducing 178
Explain, Describe, Give, and End
    Positively (EDGE) 148
Extreme Programming 16

F

failed transformation projects
  avoiding 38
  collaboration failure 39
  DevOps initiatives, management
    of expectations 40
  DevOps initiatives, rooting
    within customer values 39
  DevOps transformation
    failure, decoding 41
  iterative approach adoption failure 40
  organizational management change 39
FinOps 193, 194

G

general, value stream symbols
  Kaizen Burst 109
  operator 109
  Quality Burst 110
  Safety Stock 110
Git 159
GitOps
  development process 206, 207
  ecosystem 205, 206
  tools 207
Google Model 32

I

indirect impact
  about 133
  health of employees 133
  process dependencies 134
  shadow IT 133
information flow 106

information flow, terminology
  electronic flow 109
  Kanban Post 109
  manual flow 109
  Signal Kanban 109
information security
  significance 178, 179
Information Technology (IT) 25
infrastructure as code (IaC) 49
integrated development
    environments (IDEs) 50
integration tests 10
iterative design
  benefits 150
  processes 149
  using 150

K

Kaizen
  URL 140
Kaizen Blitz 109
Kaizen principles
  about 141
  implementing 140-142
Kanban 17
Kanplan 15, 17
key performance indicators
    (KPIs) 24, 58, 119
Kotter's change management
    model 127, 128

L

legacy infrastructure 98
legacy modernization 98, 99
lines of code (LOC) 50

M

malware 180
material flow, terminology
    inventory 109
    process 109
    shared process 109
    supplier/customer 109
Mean Time to Recovery (MTTR) 52, 232
mean time to resolution (MTTR) 168
metrics, designing for team
    large organization, with numerous
        DevOps teams 56
    medium organization, with
        advocacy team 54, 55
    scenarios 53
    small organization, with dedicated
        DevOps team 53, 54
    small organization, with outsourced
        DevOps team 57
metrics, to measure DevOps success
    about 45, 46
    common quality metrics 49, 50
    common stability metrics 51
    common velocity metrics 47
Mind Tools
    reference link 60
minimum viable product (MVP) 229

N

NoOps 29

O

objectives and key results (OKRs) 119
organizational alignment 84, 85

organizational change
    keeping pace with 151
organizational change, process steps
    about 86
    change, aligning with business goals 87
    change, defining 87
    effective support structure, providing 88
    effective training, providing 88
    impact, determining across
        organization 87
    progress, measuring 89
    strong communication strategy,
        developing 87
organizational change, roles
    about 85
    human resources (HR) 86
    management 85
owners
    defining, for tooling 187
owners of tools
    identifying, in organization 187

P

Pareto principle 113
PDCA 141
phishing 180
process change
    about 124
    business case, presenting to
        stakeholders 124
    communicating 125
    continuous improvement 126
    dependencies, evaluating 126
    final success 126
    improvement, identifying 124
    planning 125

resistance, evaluating 126
resources and data, identifying
    for evaluation 125
risk, evaluating 126
process change areas
  access, to subject matter experts 152
  effective communication 151
  knowledge transfer 152
process change, challenges
  about 134
  domino effect 136
  established goals, lacking 135
  frameworks change, need for 136
  poor strategic alignment 135
  tools, implementing 135
process change, people effects
  about 131
  direct impact 131
  indirect impact 133
processes
  changes, iterating to 149
  defining, for tooling 187
  mapping, to tools 188
process maps, versus value stream maps
  analyzing 114-116
  usage 116
product flow 107
push arrows 107

R

resistance, to change within organization
  overcoming 90, 91
  reasons 90
retrospectives 69, 70
Rogers' technology adoption
    curve 128, 129

roles and responsibilities matrix
  example 67
rollups
  creating, at organizational level 58-61
rules of engagement 68

S

Scaled Agile Framework (SAFe)
  about 19
  reference link 19
scaling up
  challenges 92
  challenges, overcoming 93, 94
Scrum 15-17
Scrumban 15, 229
Scrum Master 68
Security Assertion Markup
    Language (SAML) 182
security requirements
  about 176
Service-Level Agreements (SLAs) 5, 168
shadow IT 71, 133
silos
  breaking down, in organization 79-81
site reliability engineering (SRE) 27, 211
Six Sigma
  URL 141
S.M.A.R.T method 60
software-as-a-service (SaaS) 53
SonarQube
  URL 204
Spotify model
  used, for scaling Agile 20, 21
Static Application Security
    Testing (SAST) 204
subject-matter experts (SMEs) 60, 220

T

team structure reorganization
  about 228, 229
  chapters 230
  guilds 230, 231
  squads 229
  tribes 229, 230
terminology, value stream mapping
  cycle time 107
  lead time 107
  setup time 107
  talk time 108
  uptime 107
test-driven deployment (TDD) 50
test-driven development (TDD) 19, 28
threats
  common threats 179
  lack of confidentiality 181
  malware 180
  phishing 180
  systems offline 181
  vulnerabilities 180
time ladder 107
tooling
  focusing on 94-98
  guidelines 162-165
  owners, defining for 187
  part of process improvement,
    making 188
  processes, defining for 187
tools
  processes, mapping to 188
Toyota Production System (TPS)
  URL 141
training plans
  developing 183
  developing, for teams 185, 186

training plans, significance
  about 183
  employee engagement, increasing 184
  saving, on costs 184
  staff retention, improving 184
  staying ahead, of competitors 184
transformation anti-patterns
  about 33
  development and operations silos 34
  DevOps as tooling team 36
  DevOps team silo 34, 35
  Glorified SysAdmin 36, 37
  operations, avoiding 35
  operations, embedding 38
transformation topologies
  about 27
  container-driven topology 33
  development and operations
    collaboration 28, 29
  DevOps advocacy 31
  DevOps as a service 30
  shared operations 29
  SRE 32
transparency, DevOps culture
  about 71
  cost control 72
  disadvantages 71
  infrastructure utilization
    and efficiency 72
  verification of compliance,
    with standards 72
Travelics (fictional organization)
  current model, challenges 214
  defining 213
  future goals 214
  operating model 213, 214

U

unit tests 10
user interface tests 10

V

value stream mapping
    about 104, 110
    challenges 110, 111
    example diagram 106
    information flow 106
    other terminology 107, 108
    product flow 107
    time ladder 107
    use cases 111
    waste, identifying 112
    waste, reducing 112
value stream maps
    assessing 119
    creating 117
    current state 120, 121
    empowered team, ensuring 117
    example 117
    future state 121
    future state, designing 119
    future state, implementing 119
    problem solving, determination 117
    process, bounding 118
    process data, collecting 118
    timeline, creating 118
value stream maps, versus process maps
    analyzing 114-116
    usage 116

value stream symbols
    about 108, 109
    general 109
    information flow 109
    material flow 109
vulnerabilities
    exploiting 180

W

waste
    overproduction 113
    transport 112, 113
    waiting 113
waterfall
    about 9
    advantages 9
    disadvantages 9
work in progress (WIP) 113

X

XOps
    about 192
    approach 195
    history 192, 193
XOps landscape
    about 193
    CloudOps 194, 195
    FinOps 193, 194

Y

YAML Ain't Markup Language
    (YAML) 60

Made in the USA
Monee, IL
09 June 2022

97706892R00149